New Directions for
Institutional Research

Robert K. Toutkoushian
EDITOR-IN-CHIEF

J. Fredericks Volkwein
ASSOCIATE EDITOR

Legal Applications of Data for Institutional Research

Andrew L. Luna
EDITOR

Number 138 • Summer 2008
Jossey-Bass
San Francisco

LEGAL APPLICATIONS OF DATA FOR INSTITUTIONAL RESEARCH
Andrew L. Luna (ed.)
New Directions for Institutional Research, no. 138
Robert K. Toutkoushian, Editor-in-Chief

NEW DIRECTIONS FOR INSTITUTIONAL RESEARCH (ISSN 0271-0579, electronic ISSN 1536-075X) is part of The Jossey-Bass Higher and Adult Education Series and is published quarterly by Wiley Subscription Services, Inc., A Wiley Company, at Jossey-Bass, 989 Market Street, San Francisco, California 94103-1741 (publication number USPS 098-830). Periodicals Postage Paid at San Francisco, California, and at additional mailing offices. POSTMASTER: Send address changes to New Directions for Institutional Research, Jossey-Bass, 989 Market Street, San Francisco, California 94103-1741.

SUBSCRIPTIONS cost $85 for individuals and $209 for institutions, agencies, and libraries in the United States. See order form at end of book.

EDITORIAL CORRESPONDENCE should be sent to Robert K. Toutkoushian, Educational Leadership and Policy Studies, Education 4220, 201 N. Rose Ave., Indiana University, Bloomington, IN 47405.

New Directions for Institutional Research is indexed in *CIJE: Current Index to Journals in Education* (ERIC), *Contents Pages in Education* (T&F), and *Current Abstracts* (EBSCO).

Microfilm copies of issues and chapters are available in 16mm and 35mm, as well as microfiche in 105mm, through University Microfilms, Inc., 300 North Zeeb Road, Ann Arbor, Michigan 48106-1346.

www.josseybass.com

CONTENTS

EDITOR'S NOTES

The one true constant in law is that the law always changes. This fact is as true today as it was during the adolescent years of our country. When we study law, we do so either to win a case or to prevent one from going to court. However, as laws change, society must change in order to adapt. And as society changes, so too must laws. This never-ending cycle of change and counterchange creates in lawyers a profession that is more artisan than scientist. In 1897, Chief Justice Oliver Wendell Holmes tried to capture his thoughts on the constant transformation of law in his seminal work, "The Path of Law" (1897). In it, he argued that the life of law has not been one of logic but one of experience. This experience, he maintained, came from reports, treatises, and statutes from both the United States and England, extending back hundreds of years.

Addressing his concerns that the study of law should be bound not only by tradition and history but by a deliberate, conscious, and systematic questioning of its grounds, Holmes issued a salient assertion: "For the rational study of the law, the blackletter man may be the man of the present, but the man of the future is the man of statistics and the master of economics" (p. 469). Clearly, Holmes's prophecy has been realized as statistics and the science of probability are prevalent in all facets of our legal system today.

Because higher education has seen its share of lawsuits resulting from either intentional or unintentional actions, colleges and universities find themselves trying to defend their actions or create an environment whereby legal claims are minimized. In many instances, higher education administrators use data and statistical tools to support their arguments against discrimination or to assess the current environment within their institutions. For the most part, the institutional research office is involved, either directly or indirectly, with generating the appropriate data for administrators to use. Although it is clear that statistics are being used with greater frequency in legal proceedings, it is also true that the science of statistics and the study of law are incongruent in many ways. This seemingly incompatible nature between statistics and the law is the impetus for this volume.

As Paetzold and Willborn (2001) have stated, statistical analysis can be useful in the law only to the extent that it focuses on issues that are legally relevant to the case at hand. In other words, a great piece of statistical theory or a tried-and-true methodology may be thrown out of court if it fails to meet the rules of evidence or contradicts current legal standing. A good example of this contradiction is the use of rank in salary equity studies.

NEW DIRECTIONS FOR INSTITUTIONAL RESEARCH, no. 138, Summer 2008 © Wiley Periodicals, Inc.
Published online in Wiley InterScience (www.interscience.wiley.com) • DOI: 10.1002/ir.243

Many academic articles within higher education have asserted that rank is a discriminating factor and therefore is a tainted variable for use in salary studies. Many courts, however, disagree and force plaintiffs to prove that the rank variable is tainted before it can be removed from a model.

This volume addresses how statistics and statistical reasoning may be effectively used within the legal environment in applications pertaining to higher education and institutional research. This volume also builds on two previous *New Directions for Institutional Research* volumes. In *The Use of Data in Discrimination Issues Cases,* Rosenthal and Yancey (1985) set the foundation by editing a volume that combined both statistics and the law. Before their volume was published, little had been written about these combined concepts within higher education—and little has been written since. Although the laws have clearly changed over the past twenty-three years, the legal concerns of higher education administrators and institutional research practitioners that Rosenthal and Yancey addressed are still as strong. In 1997, Jones edited the volume *Preventing Lawsuits: The Role of Institutional Research.* Jones paved the way further for this current volume by addressing the dissimilar nature of statistics and the law and how institutional research practitioners must adapt to a new way of thinking. I hope that other volumes will continue to address the constantly changing nature of the law and how statistics can be used effectively within our legal system.

In Chapter One, I address the differences and similarities between the science of statistics and the practice of law. Although many scholars believe that the two are, for the most part, incongruent, they have to work together in preventing lawsuits or building a strong prima facie case (i.e., one that at first glance presents sufficient evidence for the plaintiff to win the case). Some statisticians may question the logic of the court's statistical reasoning, but they cannot refute the fact that these legal decisions have affected how future higher education cases may be tried. Therefore, it is important for administrators, institutional researchers, and faculty to understand the court structure, jurisdiction, and legal jurisprudence behind these cases in order to prevent lawsuits by designing campus-based studies that are statistically valid and legally sound.

Chapter Two, by Michael S. Harris and John H. Roth, focuses on the role of institutional research in enrollment management since the U.S. Supreme Court's decision in the University of Michigan affirmative action cases in 2003. This chapter explores the ways in which institutions can plan and collect data to avoid lawsuits. The authors examine the types of institutional data and decision making that the courts have ruled meet the constitutional and legal thresholds to avoid legal action.

In Chapter Three, John J. Cheslock and Suzanne E. Eckes examine the application of Title IX to intercollegiate athletics. Given the complex history of this association, they outline the policy interpretations provided by the Office for Civil Rights and relevant case law. They highlight the role of statistical evidence in demonstrating compliance and use recent data on athletic participation to describe the current level of compliance. A discussion of important economic considerations often missing from the Title IX policy debate concludes the chapter.

Bruce A. Christenson, Kathleen M. Maher, and Lorin M. Mueller address in Chapter Four the organization and maintenance of data in employment litigation. They examine the role of personnel system data in addressing allegations in employment discrimination cases and describe the types of data that are frequently relevant in assessing allegations of discrimination regarding personnel actions. Past employment discrimination cases highlight important issues related to the maintenance and organization of personnel and other organizational records. Finally, the authors consider the use of personnel data to prevent employment litigation as compared to its use at the time of litigation.

Chapter Five, by Lorin M. Mueller, Eric M. Dunleavy, and Ash K. Buonasera, examines how employment decisions like selection, promotion, and termination should be analyzed in employment discrimination litigation. This chapter combines statistical concepts with relevant case law and introduces a number of important employment discrimination concepts. It then focuses on the analysis of traditional applicant flow data using statistical significance tests including Fisher's exact test and practical significance tests such as the four-fifths rule. The chapter includes a data analytic example depicting selection decisions across two groups (for example, men and women) and reviews factors that may affect the implications of these analyses. Finally, the chapter concludes with a presentation of alternative data analytic strategies, including constructed pools analysis, that may be reasonable when traditional applicant flow data are inappropriate or unavailable.

In Chapter Six, Julie A. Frizell, Benjamin S. Shippen Jr., and I examine how compensation outcomes should be analyzed in employment discrimination litigation. The chapter addresses this issue by introducing multiple regression analysis and providing a test for discrimination, a method of compensation determination, and a procedure to calculate damages during settlement. We address potential issues associated with violations of key assumptions of the model and cite seminal and recent relevant case law in Title VII cases where regression analyses have played a significant role.

This volume explores a variety of legal issues that may affect the institutional research office. Certainly there are many more legal issues that we do not address in this volume; nevertheless, I hope that the information contained here will benefit institutional research practitioners and create a more frequent dialogue concerning the complexities of statistical science within the legal environment.

I could not have completed this volume without the dedication and hard work of each chapter author, whose expertise in this field is well noted. I also recognize the exceptional work of my graduate assistant, Anna Beth Kirk, for providing her time and talents as a proofreader. To all of these professionals, I offer my appreciation and my gratitude.

Finally, this volume is intended only as a reference on the differences and similarities of statistics and the law. It does not replace sound legal advice. For professional legal advice, consult an attorney.

Andrew L. Luna
Editor

References

Holmes, O. "The Path of Law." *Harvard Law Review*, 1897, *10*, 457–474.

Jones, L. (ed.). *Preventing Lawsuits: The Role of Institutional Research*. New Directions for Institutional Research, no. 96. San Francisco: Jossey-Bass, 1997.

Paetzold, R., and Willborn, S. *The Statistics of Discrimination: Using Statistical Evidence in Discrimination Cases*. Colorado Springs: Shepard's/McGraw-Hill, 2001.

Rosenthal, W., and Yancey, B. (eds.). *The Use of Data in Discrimination Issues Cases*. New Directions for Institutional Research, no. 48. San Francisco: Jossey-Bass, 1985.

ANDREW L. LUNA is director of institutional research, planning, and assessment at the University of North Alabama.

1

Although the practice of law and the science of statistics are often incongruent, they can and should be used together.

The Art of Combining Statistics with the Law

Andrew L. Luna

Some time ago, a company's candy bar commercial suggestively mused how its product came into existence. In the advertisement, a woman was eating chocolate and walking out a door. Coming in through the same door was a man who was eating peanut butter. As chance would have it, the two actors collided, and the chocolate accidentally found its way into the peanut butter (and vice versa). At this point the announcer commented on how two great tastes could taste great together. While it could be said that the science of statistics and the practice of law have collided together much as in this anecdote, the combined effect has left a less palatable taste in the mouths of statisticians, lawyers, and administrators.

The United States has become a litigious society, and higher education has had to answer the clarion call concerning its responsiveness to many legal issues, including discrimination, harassment, and reasonable accommodations. Since 1972, when Title VII of the 1964 Civil Rights Act was extended to cover both public and private educational institutions, numerous lawsuits have arisen out of the halls of academe. Although these court decisions have helped administrators more effectively align institutional policy within the confines of the law so that lawsuits might be minimized, lawsuits still occur quite frequently in higher education.

Furthermore, as more cases address the issue of discrimination, the courts increasingly face two distinctive problems. First, discrimination claims are more complex for faculty, staff, and students to prove and for institutions to defend against due to the subjective nature of academic

NEW DIRECTIONS FOR INSTITUTIONAL RESEARCH, no. 138, Summer 2008 © Wiley Periodicals, Inc.
Published online in Wiley InterScience (www.interscience.wiley.com) • DOI: 10.1002/ir.244

higher education (Barbezat, 2002; Kaplin and Lee, 1995). Second, the use of statistics, particularly regression analysis, is problematic for jurists and jurors alike because both have to struggle with the interpretation of statistical science and the probative value (i.e., having the effect of proving) of statistical results to the case at hand (Lempert, 1985).

There exists a rich literature on the topic of discrimination and other legal issues within higher education. Much of this work either demonstrates new statistical methodologies or tries to replicate the research from past studies. Most of it is supported by findings from previous research and cites many statistical and academic experts. What much of this work lacks, however, is a review of case law and how court decisions have defined the statistical methodologies that are recognized as a significant part of these cases. Whether this omission is due in part to the researcher's failure to understand case law or not appreciating the impact of case law on policy by not including legal decisions in published research on discrimination, this work clearly demonstrates the almost dogmatic divergence between the two disciplines. All discrimination cases, as well as many other legal issues within higher education, are based on federal law. Therefore, disregarding court decisions on this topic is not a wise administrative or academic practice because how courts interpret the law governs, to some extent, how institutions may work within it (Simpson and Rosenthal, 1982).

On the other side of the coin, lawyers seem to have trouble understanding the science of statistics and what role statistics can actually play in establishing or refuting a prima facie case of discrimination. For instance, statistical analysis has become a central means of proving discrimination in a wide variety of cases. However, statistical inference can neither prove the cause of a disparity nor identify all of the possible factors that caused the disparity (Paetzold and Willborn, 2001). Statistics should be used only as a means to provide information on the likelihood of a particular outcome.

Outside the courtroom, it has become increasingly important to study the nature and extent of certain legal problems such as faculty salary discrimination, salary compression, hiring practices, and accessibility issues and to use these studies to supply information to administrators and policymakers to either rectify a problem that may exist or to provide probative evidence if a discrimination issue is taken to court (Lee and Liu, 1999). Within the academic realm of these issues, institutional researchers have contributed significantly to the literature and have reluctantly answered the call to conduct such studies at their own institutions. When the results of an institutional salary study provide satisfactory explanations and remedies to all parties involved, the study is considered a success, and nothing further is needed. If, however, one party to an equity dispute is not satisfied with the study's results, the dispute may wind up in court, where statistical methodologies might have to yield to the procedure of law. Because institutional research practitioners and administrators are more inclined to the laws of statistical science rather

NEW DIRECTIONS FOR INSTITUTIONAL RESEARCH • DOI: 10.1002/ir

than the rules of courts, a well-crafted piece of research that replicates well-known methodologies published in respected journals may not pass the basic rules of evidence or may not be what the courts have articulated they want.

This chapter identifies the inherent differences between statistics and the law, underscores the difficulty of combining the two in cases involving higher education issues, and then addresses how the two can and should be mutually supportive of each other. When these two divergent disciplines are forced to combine and statistical evidence is introduced, conflicts often arise from misunderstandings on how lawyers and statisticians see the world. It is the intention of this chapter, as well as the rest of this volume, to increase the awareness and appreciation of how these two disciplines may work in tandem so that the scope and potential of both may be more fully realized.

Law of Discrimination

Most lawsuits involving colleges and universities concern discrimination in some way. Therefore, the focus of this chapter is on issues pertaining to discrimination. Essentially there exist two basic models of discrimination: one focuses on the intentions of the decision makers and the other on the criteria decision makers use (Paetzold and Willborn, 2001). Although harassment and reasonable accommodation are somewhat different from these two models, they were derived from them. Because the focus of this volume is discrimination law, it is important to understand the relevant laws and how they affect higher education.

Two statutes exist on which claims of discrimination in employment are filed: the Equal Pay Act and Title VII of the 1964 Civil Rights Act. Currently faculty members use both statutes to dispute pay disparities in higher education. It is important to understand that there are only two ways in which a federal law may change: through legislative act or the interpretation of the court dealing with a particular point of law in a case. The legislature created both the Equal Pay Act and the Civil Rights Act of 1964. Over the years, however, the courts have made various changes to the law through their function of interpretation (Wren and Wren, 1986).

Equal Pay Act. When a male and a female employee perform job functions that are substantially equal but receive different salaries, the Equal Pay Act is often used to decide if discrimination exists. The statute prohibits employers from paying unequal wages to people working jobs that "require equal skill, effort, and responsibility and which are performed under similar working conditions, except where such payment is made pursuant to (i) a seniority system, (ii) a merit system (iii) a system which measures earnings by quantity or quality of production, or (iv) a differential based on any other factor other than sex" (29 U.S.C. sec. 206(d)(1)).

The U.S. Supreme Court has established a two-step process for evaluating an Equal Pay Act claim. First, the plaintiff must prove a violation by showing that the skill, efforts, and responsibility required in performance of the jobs are substantially equal. Once the plaintiff makes a prima facie case, the employer then has the opportunity to show that the pay differential was due to one of the four affirmative defenses listed above (*County of Washington* v. *Gunter*, 1981).

Title VII of the Civil Rights Act of 1964. When the job structure within a business or institution is substantially segregated by sex, race, or ethnicity, and workers of any suspect class are paid less than other workers who perform the work that is of comparable value or worth to their employer, the lower-paid worker may file a claim under Title VII. This statute is considered the most comprehensive and therefore has been the most frequently used of the federal employment discrimination laws. In 1972, the statute was extended to cover public and private educational institutions, and today it is the most used discrimination statute within higher education.

Title VII essentially has two parts. The first part stipulates that it shall be unlawful for an employer "to fail or refuse to hire or to discharge any individual, or otherwise to discriminate against any individual with respect to his compensation, terms, conditions, or privileges or employment, because of such individual's race, color, religion, sex, or national origin." The next section makes it unlawful for an employer "to limit, segregate, or classify his employees or applicants for employment in any way which would deprive or tend to deprive any individual of employment opportunities or otherwise adversely affect his status as an employee because of such individual's race, color, religion, sex, or national origin" (42 U.S.C sec. 2000e-2(h)). The major exception to this statute is a bona-fide occupational qualification (BFOQ) that is necessary to the normal operation of a business or enterprise. For example, gender could be a BFOQ in an all-male residence hall, and religion could be a BFOQ at a religiously affiliated college or university. Two legal models are used in defining and establishing a Title VII case.

The disparate impact model concerns employment practices that are "fair in form but discriminatory in operation" (*Griggs* v. *Duke Power Co.*, 1971, p. 424). The employer does not need to have any intent to discriminate; rather, some presumably neutral policy of the employer has a discriminatory impact on the claimants or the class of person they represent (Kaplin and Lee, 1995). In its unanimous opinion in *Griggs*, the U.S. Supreme Court created a two-step process for establishing a prima facie case under the disparate impact model. The court prohibited employment practices that (1) operate to exclude or otherwise discriminate against employees or prospective employees on grounds of race, color, religion, sex, or national origin and (2) are unrelated to job performance or not justified by business necessity. Under this model, both requirements must be met before Title VII is violated.

The disparate treatment model involves intentional discrimination with a discriminatory motive, and, under a class action suit, the evidence must establish a pattern, practice, or custom of discrimination (*Barnett* v. *Grant*, 1975). The U.S. Supreme Court established a three-step process for evaluating a disparate treatment claim. First, the plaintiffs bear the burden of establishing a prima facie case of discrimination by a preponderance of the evidence (*McDonnell Douglas Corp.* v. *Green*, 1973; *Texas Department of Community Affairs* v. *Burdine*, 1981). Second, once they have done so, the burden shifts to the defendant to articulate some legitimate, nondiscriminatory reason for the challenged employment practice (*McDonnell Douglas Corp.* v. *Green*, 1973). In cases where the plaintiff has relied on statistical evidence to establish a prima facie case of discrimination, the defendants may also attempt to undermine the plaintiff's prima facie case by attacking the validity of that statistical evidence or introducing statistical evidence of their own showing that the challenged practice did not result in disparate treatment (*Berger* v. *Iron Workers Reinforced Rodmen Local 201*, 1988; *International Brotherhood of Teamsters* v. *U.S.*, 1977). Third, if the defendants meet this burden, the plaintiffs must then show either that the defendants' statistical proof is inadequate or that the defendants' explanation for the challenged practice is merely a pretext for discrimination (*Zahorik* v. *Cornell University*, 1984).

Understanding case law and how statistical evidence applies to it may be an important step in preventing salary discrimination lawsuits on campus (Simpson and Rosenthal, 1982). Information gained from case law may allow administrators, institutional researchers, and faculty to more effectively plan and conduct gender salary equity studies on their campuses, using the results to help account for any unexplained salary variations and allow the institution to properly remedy any salary disparities that may exist within the context of current legal jurisprudence. An understanding of case law will also aid in preparing a more legally sound statistical model if a salary dispute goes to court.

The Structure of the Courts

Within the U.S. judicial system are several levels of courts, each performing a specific function. The federal courts, where most salary equity cases are tried, have three levels: the district or trial court, the intermediate appellate or circuit court, and the final appellate or U.S. Supreme Court. The U.S. judicial system consists of eighty-four district courts and thirteen circuit courts of appeals. District courts cover a specific geographical area within a particular state that is based on that area's population. With the exception of the District of Columbia and federal circuit, each circuit court of appeals encompasses several states. Within each of the first two judicial levels, the courts act independently of each other. In other words, the decisions and interpretations by the U.S. Court of Appeals for the Fourth Circuit in one case may contradict the decisions and interpretations of the U.S. Court of Appeals for the Second Circuit in a similar case.

The trial or lower court's responsibility is to collect evidence from both parties, determine how that evidence relates to the law, and make a decision based on the court's conclusions of the evidence and interpretation of the law. The job of the appellate court is to ensure that the trial court applied the relevant and appropriate points of law to the evidence provided. Very rarely do appellate courts reevaluate or redetermine findings of facts made at the trial level (Wren and Wren, 1986).

At this point, it is important to distinguish between case precedents that are mandatory and those that are persuasive. Mandatory precedent cases are those from the highest court within that particular jurisdiction. Because most discrimination cases involve federal law, the U.S. Supreme Court is the highest court in the federal jurisdiction. Persuasive cases come from lower federal courts and are used as guidance to other cases (Wren and Wren, 1986). For example, district court decisions, as well as other appellate court decisions, are persuasive only to another appellate court. Appellate court decisions, however, are mandatory within the circuit where they reside. And cases decided by the U.S. Supreme Court create mandatory precedent that each district and appellate court must follow. If, however, there are inconsistent decisions coming from the federal appellate courts, the U.S. Supreme Court may be compelled to make a decision on one of these cases so that a mandatory precedent may be established. Therefore, appellate court decisions are considered the law of the land for the circuit where they reside, and U.S. Supreme Court decisions are considered the law of the land for the country.

What Is Fair Versus What Is Legal

Before a discrimination issue has the chance to leave the halls of academe and go to court, it is wise for the administration to investigate all allegations and redress any inequities, if apparent, no matter how significant the financial burden is on the institution (Boudreau and others, 1997). Furthermore, Braskamp, Muffo, and Langston (1978) argue that any fair review of discrimination issues requires a clear definition of the policies on campus and how these policies are related to professional experiences, scholarly achievements, instructional effectiveness, and service. During this type of analysis, however, the use of basic human judgment and what may or may not be fair often weighs in heavily on both administrators and faculty (Moore, 1993).

On one side of the human equation process exists history and the argument that many studies have shown compelling evidence, and courts have agreed, that discrimination does exist among particular classes of people (Barbezat, 2002). On the other side of the equation exists the argument that the judgment of whether inequities exist should be answered by the distinct fields of law, economics, and statistics (Moore, 1993).

In some instances, legal decisions on discrimination may not correlate to what faculty or administrators believe to be justifiable arguments based on human capital theories or statistical studies. In some cases, court decisions have even redefined well-established statistical measures and practices. Furthermore, some legal scholars have argued that the methods of proving discrimination through statistical models are based on faulty statistical and factual assumptions and misconceived interpretations of the meaning of statistical evidence (Browne, 1993). This often-strong dichotomy of reasoning between legal scholars and statistical and economical scientists is the main argument as to why discrimination disputes should be settled within the institution and should never wind up in court. Essentially when the courts review quantitative evidence on a discrimination issue, it is not to develop a general theory of human behavior but to decide which evidence is legally stronger in order to settle a dispute (Simpson and Rosenthal, 1982).

When court decisions are rendered, many have been questioned as to how fair or just they are, and discrimination cases are not immune to this type of inquiry. It should be noted that while an institution may be compelled to follow a particular court decision concerning discrimination, such a decision should not automatically prevent administrators from further investigating the fairness of its employment structure or move beyond the law in their quest for a more equitable structure. It should also be noted, however, that statistics are only part of the court's analysis of a case. Courts use law, the experience of the jurists, and intuition as guides in the resolution of a case (Baldus and Cole, 1980).

Statistics and the Courts

Although statistics and the legal system are almost dichotomous in theory, in practice the courts have nonetheless acknowledged the use of statistics in discrimination cases, albeit slowly. In 1973, the U.S. Supreme Court established the basic analytical framework for providing an individual case of intentional discrimination, or disparate treatment, under Title VII. The Court stated that the plaintiff could prove unlawful discrimination, and once the showing has been made, an employer must articulate a legitimate, nondiscriminatory reason in order to avoid liability (*McDonnell Douglas Corp.* v. *Green,* 1973). This decision induced plaintiffs and defendants alike to use statistics as part of their probative evidence. Soon after its decision, courts were obligated to recognize an increase of statistical evidence in discrimination cases. In *Hazelwood School District* v. *U.S.* (1977), the Court clarified the use of statistics in Title VII cases by stating that the government could establish a prima facie case of race discrimination by the use of statistics. The U.S. Supreme Court's decision in *International Brotherhood of Teamsters* v. *U.S.* (1977) further confirmed the use of statistics in discrimination cases when it held that statistics are probative of discrimination, especially when they are combined with anecdotal evidence. As we will later see, courts have had to rely solely on anecdotal evidence when the statistical models used become either too complex or esoteric.

In addition to what the courts have said, the Federal Rules of Evidence define as relevant all "evidence having any tendency to make the existence of any fact that is of consequence to the determination of the action more probable or less probable than it would be without the evidence" (Federal Rules of Evidence, 401, 2001). Moreover, these rules indicate two grounds by which statistical evidence may be excluded if it fails to be statistically significant. The first, Rule 703 (Federal Rules of Evidence, 703, 2001), provides that the evidence must be "of a type reasonably relied upon by in the particular field in forming opinions or inferences upon the subject." Second, Rule 403 (Federal Rules of Evidence, 403, 2001) states that all relevant evidence may be excluded if its probative value is substantially outweighed by its tendency to waste time, confuse the issues, or mislead the jury. As Toutkoushian and Hoffman (2002) stated, a wide range of statistical methods for measuring wage disparity exists, each having varying levels of complexity and difficulty. Although the authors stress that the type of model used is based in part on how the research results will be used, it is also clear that the courts may find that the simpler single-equation model satisfies Rule 403 more than the multiple-equation methods will. However, this assumption has yet to be directly tested.

Since 1977, when the U.S. Supreme Court became more receptive to the use of statistics, lower federal courts have struggled with the significance and probative value of statistics in discrimination cases, as well as to their admissibility in general. This result of the struggle for jurists to understand statistics has been courts from different jurisdictions simultaneously interpreting statistics differently. Currently many of these cases can be used by model developers to understand judicial thinking regarding statistics. As the U.S. Supreme Court hears more cases involving statistical methodologies, a narrower definition and scope of the role of statistics and their interpretation will clearly result.

The Logical Dilemma Between Law and Statistics

Many scholars believe the science of statistics and the practice of law are, for the most part, incongruent. When statistical evidence is introduced, conflicts arise due to the gaps between statistical and legal reasoning. These differences evolve from the significant way in which statisticians and lawyers differ in their view of the world and are defined by Paetzold and Willborn (2001): *The language of statistics is uncertainty, while the language of law is certainty.* In other words, statistical evidence should only approve or reject a null hypothesis rather than prove it. At best, statistical tests can only support that something either happened or did not happen by chance. In contrast, the preponderance of evidence in a court of law is used to "prove" someone's guilt or innocence no matter what the actual truth may be. This language can cause confusion because courts may refer to their decisions as proof, but in reality they are not proving guilt or innocence but instead drawing conclusions based upon the preponderance of the evidence, in much the same way as traditional hypothesis testing does not prove or dis-prove a null hypothesis. Throughout the history of the U.S. Judiciary, there are stories about guilty people who were found innocent and *vice versa.* Therefore, the court becomes uncomfortable with the uncertainty of statistical inference, but for statisticians, it is a fact of life.

Statistical methodologies and the philosophy of statistics are mainly based on deductive reasoning, while the practice of law is mainly based on inductive reasoning. Deductive reasoning is the process by which someone makes conclusions based on previously known facts—for instance, all oranges are fruit, and all fruit grows on trees, and therefore all oranges grow on trees. Contrary to deductive reasoning, inductive reasoning is the process of arriving at a conclusion based on a set of observations. For example, the flame is hot, so all flames are hot. The ball goes up in the air when kicked, so all balls that are kicked go up in the air. Inductive reasoning, however, may not be a valid method of proof. Just because someone observes a number of situations in which a pattern exists does not mean that the pattern is true for all occasions.

Lawyers use data they only need to prove a case, while the practice of statistics requires the use of all pertinent data, and any anomalies must be identified. Whereas the vast majority of attorneys live by their profession's ethical codes, they are still (and should be) biased to their clients whom they are representing. This bias is the antithesis to the ethical codes of statisticians, who are required to use what data are needed in order to complete the analysis.

The statistician may view evidence inconclusively, while the lawyer is obligated to view evidence decisively. The practice of statistics is based on the probability of occurrence by chance or by special cause of variation. Even if there is a high probability that $A = B$, in some cases, this will be a faulty conclusion. In a legal hearing, only two outcomes exist: a jury is instructed to convict or not convict based on the preponderance of the evidence and through the subjective measure of reasonable doubt. The court does not have the luxury of waiting for further evidence that could possibly become available.

In law, what is considered proof follows a well-defined standard based on the preponderance of evidence or facts at hand. In statistics, the nature of truth is always probabilistic. In law, the standard of proof is subjective and depends on the nature of the case. Here, the attorney is interested in submitting as much evidence as he or she is allowed to submit to prove or refute a case. In statistics, the scientist has to be concerned with the fact that all occurrences have variability and error and should be reported that way.

Statistical jargon may confuse jurists, whereas legal jargon may confuse statisticians. It is no secret that both attorneys and statisticians have terminology that does not easily transfer to the other's discipline. Statistical jargon confounds attorneys, and legal jargon baffles statisticians. Caught in the middle are jurors, who are equally confused and frustrated by both.

On the face of it, attorneys have rules and laws they must obey, and the preference they show to their clients is clearly demonstrated in the evidence

NEW DIRECTIONS FOR INSTITUTIONAL RESEARCH • DOI: 10.1002/ir

they present. Although attorneys who use research in court cases may not intentionally bias statistical results, partiality to a particular statistical finding may still be implied (Simpson and Rosenthal, 1982). For instance, according to Hunt (1979), "Almost never do you see a researcher who appears as an independent witness, quite unbiased. You almost always see a witness appearing either for the [Federal Trade Commission] FTC or for the industry. You can almost predict what is going to be concluded by the witness for the FTC. And you can almost predict what will be concluded by the witness for industry. That says that research in this setting is not after full truth and it is not dispassionate in nature" (p. 152).

Although statistical evidence is valuable, it can also be misleading because of the difference between the legal definition of *discrimination* and the statistical translation underlying statistical inference. According to Paetzold and Willborn (2001), whenever statistical evidence is used, three types of models contribute to the inferential process: the legal model, which determines how evidence can be used in court; the situational model, which focuses on either the intentions of the employer or the actual criteria employers used in the employment process, or both; and the statistical model, which consists of the formal rules and methodologies that guide the scientific process.

Because of the nature of research, statistical evidence cannot prove discrimination actually exists. It can only show that a probability may exist whereby an institutional standard of employment is beyond the boundaries of chance occurrence. Therefore, when the statistical model indicates a potential deviation from the norm, it is up to the lawyers to incorporate the other two models within the inferential process to determine whether it is more likely than not that discrimination occurred (Paetzold and Willborn, 2001). When this happens, the objective nature of statistics may be overwhelmed by the rules of evidence, attorney-client bias, or circumstantial evidence.

To show how the reasoning of statistical inference may be contradictory to the practice of law, consider the measurement of height and Sir Francis Galton. Galton, cousin to Charles Darwin, first used the term *regression* to support his theory that taller fathers tended to have shorter sons, and shorter fathers tended to have taller sons. In other words, the height of fathers' sons tended to regress toward the mean. Using a regression analysis in this manner would create a statistical inference to the height of a son based in part on the height of the father or mother, or both.

Suppose that a woman gives birth to a child. She is five feet four inches tall, and her husband is five feet seven inches tall. Let us further suppose that according to a statistical table that was determined after running a point-in-time regression model of thousands of parents, the fully grown son's height would fall within five feet five inches and six feet one inch if it is to be within acceptable standards of random variation. If the son's actual height is significantly over or under this range, it becomes a significant deviation from normal. According to statistical reasoning, this variation could be attributed to a special cause or causes, it could signal an outlier with no apparent specific cause, or there could be enough error in the model to induce the researcher to falsely reject the null hypothesis.

If this height variation were submitted as evidence in court, the legal, situational, and statistical models described by Paetzold and Willborn (2001) would be scrutinized to establish a prima facie case against the mother indicating that her husband was not the father of her son. The burden of proof would then fall on the mother to show beyond a reasonable doubt that her husband was in fact the actual father. In this case, the attorney for the mother may incorporate statistical evidence consisting of a longitudinal regression analysis that may refute the claim. Unless her evidence is significantly compelling, the woman may be found guilty of promiscuity simply because her legally forced burden to prove her husband was the real father may be beyond the capabilities of statistical inference. This example may sound extraordinary, but it may not be.

Many courts have recognized that excluding chance as a factor is not the same as determining the occurrence of impermissible discrimination; other courts, however, do not understand the difference and are not so careful. In *Palmer* v. *George P. Shultz* (1987), the court stated, "Nor can statistics determine, if chance is an unlikely explanation, whether the more probable cause was intentional discrimination or a legitimate nondiscriminatory factor in the selection process (p. 90)." In *Maddox* v. *Claytor* (1985), the court concurred, stating that "it is important to stress that a disparity translating into a large number of standard deviations does not automatically point to discrimination as the cause" (p. 1552).

Contrary to these decisions, in *Payne* v. *Travenol Lab, Inc.* (1982, p. 820), the court stated, "Absent explanation, standard deviation of greater than three generally signals discrimination . . ." In *Ivy* v. *Meridian Coca-Cola Bottling Co.* (1986, p. 157), the court decided in part that "a fluctuation of two or three standard deviations indicates that the result is caused by discriminatory intent rather than chance." Likewise, in *Rivera* v. *City of Wichita Falls* (1982, p. 532), the court stated that "standard deviation analysis quantifies the likelihood of a benign explanation for an observed discrepancy . . ."

Conclusion

The object of statistical hypothesis testing is simply to determine if the deviation of a variable is within the realm of chance occurrence or if there is a significant probability that the deviation is beyond the boundaries of chance. While this testing is still stronger and more empirical than the legal standard of weighing a verdict on the preponderance of the evidence, there are still flaws in using statistical evidence as proof of the existence or absence of discrimination. Just because there may exist a disproportionately and significantly higher rate of one class of people who get jobs, promotions, raises, and so on over another group of qualified candidates does not automatically mean that an institution is acting in a discriminatory way.

NEW DIRECTIONS FOR INSTITUTIONAL RESEARCH • DOI: 10.1002/ir

However, because of the apparent misunderstanding of some courts as to the true nature of statistical reasoning, evidence from a plaintiff that is considered statistically significant forcibly closes the doors on the defendant to show chance cause for the disparity. The defendant then has to prove that beyond a reasonable doubt, there is either no disparity or that the apparent disparity is not caused by illegal discrimination. Many institutions have argued that to ensure there is no statistically significant disparity between groups of people, a quota system must be in place that, if implemented, would go against both the spirit and the letter of the Equal Pay Act and Title VII.

Although there are no clear-cut answers to these here, it is clear that a greater understanding of the relationship between statistics and the law should be sought and that institutional research practitioners may be best suited to effectively blend these divergent philosophies into a more useful and coherent resource.

References

Baldus, D., and Cole, J. *Statistical Proof of Discrimination.* New York: McGraw-Hill, 1980.

Barbezat, D. "History of Pay Equity Studies." In R. Toutkoushian (ed.), *Conducting Salary-Equity Studies: Alternative Approaches to Research.* New Directions for Institutional Research, no. 115. San Francisco: Jossey-Bass, 2002.

Barnett v. Grant, 518 F.2d 54 (1975).

Berger v. Iron Workers Reinforced Rodmen Local 201, 269 U.S. app. D.C. 67 (1988).

Boudreau, N., and others. "Should Faculty Rank Be Included as a Predictor Variable in Studies of Gender Equity in University Faculty Salaries?" *Research in Higher Education,* 1997, *38*(3), 297–312.

Braskamp, L., Muffo, J., and Langston, I. "Determining Salary Equity: Politics, Procedures, and Problems." *Journal of Higher Education,* 1978, *49*, 231–246.

Browne, K. "Statistical Proof of Discrimination: Beyond 'Damned Lies.'" *Washington Law Review,* 1993, *68*, 477–558.

County of Washington v. Gunter, 452 U.S. 161 (1981).

Federal Rules of Evidence, 401. (2001).

Federal Rules of Evidence, 403. (2001).

Federal Rules of Evidence, 703. (2001).

Griggs v. Duke Power Company, 401 U.S. 424 (1971).

Hazelwood School District v. U.S., 433 U.S. 399 (1977).

Hunt, H. "The Ethics of Research in the Common Interest." In N. Ackerman (ed.), "Panel Summary." In *Proceedings of the American Council of Consumer Interests Conference.* Milwaukee, 1979.

International Brotherhood of Teamsters v. U.S., 431 U.S. 324 (1977).

Ivy v. Meridian Coca-Cola Bottling Co., 641 F. Supp. 157 (1986).

Kaplin, W., and Lee, B. *Law in Higher Education.* San Francisco: Jossey-Bass, 1995.

Lee, J., and Liu, C. "Measuring Discrimination in the Workplace: Strategies for Lawyers and Policymakers." *University of Chicago Law School Roundtable,* 1999, *6*, 195–234.

Lempert, R. "Symposium on Law and Economics: Statistics in the Courtroom." *Columbia Law Review,* 1985, *85*, 1098–1116.

Maddox v. Claytor, 764 F.2d 1539 (1985).

McDonnell Douglas Corp. v. Green, 411 U.S. 792 (1973).

Moore, N. "Faculty Salary Equity: Issues in Model Selection." *Research in Higher Education,* 1993, *34*, 107–125.

NEW DIRECTIONS FOR INSTITUTIONAL RESEARCH • DOI: 10.1002/ir

Paetzold, R., and Willborn, S. *The Statistics of Discrimination: Using Statistical Evidence in Discrimination Cases*. Colorado Springs: Shepard's/McGraw-Hill, 2001.

Palmer v. George P. Shultz, 815 F.2d 84 (1987).

Payne v. Travenol Lab., Inc., 673 F.2d 798 (1982).

Rivera v. City of Wichita Falls, 655 F.2d 531 (1982).

Simpson, W., and Rosenthal, W. "The Role of the Institutional Researcher in a Sex Discrimination Suit." *Research in Higher Education*, 1982, *16*, 3–26.

Texas Department of Community Affairs v. Burdine, 450 U.S. 248 (1981).

Toutkoushian, R., and Hoffman, E. "Alternatives for Measuring the Unexplained Wage Gap." In R. Toutkoushian (ed.), *Conducting Salary-Equity Studies: Alternative Approaches to Research*. New Directions for Institutional Research, no. 115. San Francisco: Jossey-Bass, 2002.

Wren, C., and Wren, J. *The Legal Research Manual: A Game Plan for Legal Research and Analysis*. (2nd ed.). Madison, Wis.: Adams & Ambrose, 1986.

Zahorik v. Cornell University, 729 F.2d 85 (1984).

ANDREW L. LUNA is director of institutional research, planning, and assessment at the University of North Alabama.

2

The courts have ruled as to what types of institutional data and decision making meet constitutional and legal thresholds to avoid legal action.

The Use of Data in Affirmative Action Litigation

Michael S. Harris, John H. Roth

The debate surrounding minority access to higher education in the United States can be traced back to the response of W.E.B. DuBois to Booker T. Washington's call for industrial education for the newly freed people following the Civil War. A product of higher education at Fisk and Harvard universities, DuBois fiercely advocated that black youth could advance further through education according to their academic abilities as the means for improving the black community. The often volatile debate surrounding how best to improve the position of minorities in American society has continued unabated since the debate between Washington and DuBois. Affirmative action programs have been in place on college and university campuses for more than forty years. The goal of these programs has been to increase the participation in higher education of underrepresented minorities and, as a result, improve the diversity of campuses and enrich the educational experience of all students. The question of access is a critical debate on the most selective of university campuses where competitive admission policies limit student enrollment (Bowen and Bok, 1998).

The U.S. Supreme Court's decisions in 2003 in the affirmative action cases of *Gratz* v. *Bollinger* (2003) and *Grutter* v. *Bollinger* (2003), sometimes referred to as the "Michigan cases," provided the first indication of the role that race-conscious admission policies will play in higher education in the new century since the Court's decision twenty-five years earlier in *Regents of the University of California* v. *Bakke* (1978). Following the *Bakke* decision but prior to the Court's ruling in the Michigan cases, the conflicts between

NEW DIRECTIONS FOR INSTITUTIONAL RESEARCH, no. 138, Summer 2008   © Wiley Periodicals, Inc.
Published online in Wiley InterScience (www.interscience.wiley.com) • DOI: 10.1002/ir.245

19

the decisions of various appellate courts, including *Hopwood* v. *Texas,* (1996) and *Smith* v. *University of Washington Law School* (2000), muddled much of the legal affirmative action debate nationally.

This chapter examines the Court's decisions in the Michigan cases and provides recommendations for institutional researchers and other administrators to assist their campuses in complying with recent court decisions while preparing for the inevitable next round of litigation. Before turning to the details of the legal history of affirmative action and our recommendations, we first examine the idea of diversity in higher education.

Benefits of Diversity in Higher Education

A number of scholars argue that diversity can have a "transformative effect" on colleges and universities, influencing "who is taught, what is taught, and who teaches" (Milem, 2003, p. 145; Chang, 1999). From a legal perspective, promoting diversity on campus has been widely considered a compelling state interest of public colleges and universities since Supreme Court Justice Lewis Powell's opinion in the seminal 1978 *Bakke* decision. As a result of *Bakke,* race-conscious admissions policies were considered constitutional provided they were narrowly tailored and could withstand a strict scrutiny review. In *Bakke,* as well as *Grutter* and *Gratz,* the use of research to support the benefits of diversity was important in the final decisions.

In this section, we review the research in support of diversity before turning to the specifics of the applicable case law on affirmative action in higher education. Two significant bodies of the literature are important to understanding the educational benefits of diversity. The first area examines the ways in which institutions promote engagement with diversity through programmatic and curricular efforts. A second area explores the interactions between students that occur largely without direct institutional influence and often outside the classroom.

An institutional commitment to diversity and the fostering of an ethos of inclusion may hold powerful influence over students. Whitt and others (2001) contend that simply accepting students and creating structural or statistical diversity does not always produce appreciable educational benefits. Creating a campus climate supportive of students from diverse backgrounds and views is essential and can improve the openness of students to perspectives different from their own. This type of environment assists in achieving the advantages of diversity on college and university campuses. The literature in support of diversity also supports linkages between academic benefits such as improved problem-solving skills and an increase of diversity within the classroom (Gurin, 1999; Terenzini and others, 2001). Studies show that the benefits can exist across all races and ethnicities, not simply those minorities whose race may have been a factor during their application for admission to the institution. Milem's work (2003) shows that the majority of students with no previous direct exposure to minority peers gain the most from diversity in the classroom.

The historical argument in support of affirmative action efforts in college admissions, which has always been problematic for many, is the ability to remedy past discrimination. The classroom education benefits rationale moves the debate away from past discrimination to the current tangible advantages of diversity. Chang (1999) found an additional benefit of diversity to higher education institutions to be the positive effect on student retention, a vital issue for colleges and universities, particularly in the modern era of accountability. This finding is significant to supporting diversity in admissions: increased amounts of structural diversity on campus lead to increasing levels of student retention. The academic mission and aims of higher education in admitting, retaining, and producing highly successful graduates does not simply support the need for a diverse student population for social justice reasons—though social justice is critical to the historical role of higher education as a vehicle for social mobility in the United States. The research literature in support of diversity also supports a significant quantity and quality of interaction (Gurin, Dey, Hurtado, and Gurin, 2002).

The addition of a diversity course requirement in the undergraduate general education curriculum and the broader expansion of multicultural elements in university courses have changed the classroom experience of today's college students (Chang, 2002). As important as the curricular additions are to expanding an appreciation of diversity, the role of students' experiences outside the classroom influences their development both academically and socially (Pascarella and Terenzini, 1991). These experiences take place in a variety of settings across campus, from interactions in the residence halls to conversations in the cafeteria, to athletic competition on the intramural field. As Piaget (1965) demonstrates, different perspectives are important for intellectual and moral development. Without a variety of views and backgrounds on campus, students are not presented with challenges to their current understandings or the limitations of their viewpoints. The cognitive development that occurs when meeting, discussing, and interacting with difference is a major component of the development necessary to function in an increasingly global society. Gurin, Dey, Hurtado, and Gurin (2002) add a much needed theoretical rationale to diversity research. They expand on the growing body of literature regarding the benefits of education by considering statistical data from an institutional and national longitudinal study to demonstrate the importance of diverse populations on campus.

The research literature on the educational benefits of diversity is derived from different methodological approaches and data sources (Gurin, Dey, Hurtado, and Gurin, 2002). The results of these studies demonstrate the potential benefits to students, faculty, and institutions. Much of the historical debate surrounding affirmative action and race-conscious admissions policies has centered on anecdotal or poorly validated rationales on both sides. Research particularly over the last ten years has provided sound data for the University of Michigan and its supporters to argue the benefits of diversity.

Legal History of Affirmative Action in Admissions

In this section, we discuss the major events in the history of affirmative action in the legal setting and detail the two affirmative action cases from the University of Michigan.

Regents of the University of California v. *Bakke.* The legal justification for the constitutionality of affirmative action programs is predicated on the notion that such programs serve a compelling government interest of the institution and broader society. The equal protection clause of the Fourteenth Amendment to the U.S. Constitution broadly provides, "No State shall . . . deny to any person within its jurisdiction the equal protection of the laws." This protection, of course, applies to all races, whether minority or majority in number. Stated another way, "The guarantee of equal protection cannot mean one thing when applied to one individual and something else when applied to a person of another color. If both are not accorded the same protection, then it is not equal" (*Bakke*, pp. 289–290). Where admissions criteria are based on racial and ethnic distinctions, therefore, such criteria are "immediately suspect" and, accordingly, "call for the most exacting judicial examination" (*Bakke*, p. 291). Justice Powell's landmark opinion in *Regents of the University of California* v. *Bakke* established the legal precedent of using race as a factor in satisfying the government's interest in diversity. In *Bakke,* the Court held that quotas or other rigid numerical systems are unconstitutional, yet allowed the use of race as a "plus" factor in making admissions decisions. That is, race and ethnicity could be a factor, but not the deciding factor. The admissions process could allow the consideration of race equal with that of all other aspects of determining the qualifications of an applicant. Justice Powell found the need for a diverse student population persuasive due to the benefits diversity brings to the educational process and future success of graduates.

The *Bakke* case began when Allan Bakke, a Caucasian male, was twice denied admission to the medical school at the University of California at Davis. After the second denial, Bakke filed suit against the school in the Superior Court of California, alleging that the school's special admissions program caused him to be denied his rights under the equal protection clause. The issue in question was the school's racial set-aside admissions program, whereby a set number of seats in each entering class were reserved for members of certain minority groups. Although in Justice Powell's opinion, student body diversity is a compelling state interest that can justify the use of race in college and university admissions, the *Bakke* Court ultimately invalidated the set-aside program. In his opinion, Justice Powell rejected three arguments presented in favor of the racial set-aside: promoting an interest in reducing the "historic deficit of traditionally disfavored minorities in medical schools and in the medical profession" (*Bakke,* pp. 306–307), remedying societal discrimination, and "increasing the number of physicians who will practice in communities currently underserved" (p. 306). Justice Powell, however, approved the use of race in admissions decisions based on an interest in promoting diversity in the student body, with the important caveat that "constitutional limitations protecting individual rights may not be disregarded" (*Bakke,* p. 311). As Justice Powell opined, "The nation's future depends upon leaders trained through wide exposure to the ideas and mores of students as diverse as this Nation of many peoples" (p. 312).

Unfortunately for practitioners, the *Bakke* decision was a fractured one: four justices concluded that the program was constitutional, and four concluded that it was unconstitutional, with Justice Powell casting the deciding vote and ultimately delivering the judgment of the Court. Because Justice Powell's opinion was not joined by any other justices of the Court, many courts struggled during the twenty-five years following *Bakke* with the question of whether the standards announced by Justice Powell in *Bakke* constitute binding precedent. Much of the litigation following the *Bakke* decision has relied on Justice Powell's opinion, the complicated aspects of which have led to much legal indecision (*Grutter* v. *Bollinger,* 2003). Although Justice Powell's opinion in *Bakke* was not joined by a majority of the justices of the Court, it provides a substantial justification for the use of race in college admissions. In fact, "most colleges and universities with affirmative action admissions plans followed the Powell guidelines" (Kaplin and Lee, 2006, p. 788).

Hopwood v. Texas. Although the U.S. Supreme Court has found affirmative action to be illegal in several opinions outside higher education following *Bakke,* the first most significant higher education affirmative action case following *Bakke* is the 1996 decision in *Hopwood* v. *Texas.* In *Hopwood,* the Fifth Circuit Court of Appeals examined the constitutionality of using race as a factor in the admissions process and held the University of Texas Law School's admission process to be unconstitutional because a separate review occurred for majority and minority applicants. In the *Hopwood* court's opinion, preferential treatment and separate qualifications were applied based on the race and ethnicity of applicants, which, it believed, violated the equal protection clause. Furthermore, the *Hopwood* court ruled that despite Justice Powell's opinion in *Bakke,* diversity was not a compelling government interest. The *Hopwood* decision therefore prevented the use of race within the Fifth Circuit, which includes the states of Texas, Mississippi, and Louisiana. However, because the U.S. Supreme Court chose not to hear an appeal from the *Hopwood* decision, the *Hopwood* decision was the controlling authority in the Fifth Circuit only.

Smith v. University of Washington Law School. In 2002, the Ninth Circuit Court of Appeals considered the case of *Smith* v. *University of Washington Law School.* In *Smith,* plaintiffs were assisted by the Center for Individual Rights, which had successfully supported the *Hopwood* case. The plaintiffs in *Smith* contended that the law school's admissions process was not narrowly tailored and used race as a deciding factor. In response, the law school argued for the benefits of educational diversity and that its affirmative action program satisfied the strict scrutiny standard of review announced by Justice Powell in *Bakke*. The *Smith* court agreed with the university that diversity was a compelling government interest, thereby disagreeing with the decision in *Hopwood*. Therefore, the *Smith* decision allowed the use of race within the Ninth Circuit, which comprises the states of Alaska, Arizona, California, Hawaii, Idaho, Montana, Nevada, Oregon, and Washington.

Resolution of Circuit Court Conflicts. Under the American judicial system, appellate court decisions constitute binding law only within the geographical region over which the appellate court has jurisdiction. The law of one circuit may merely be compelling authority in another circuit. As a result, different rulings may occur in various circuits, such that what the law is in Texas may not be the law in Washington. Inconsistent rulings across different circuits therefore can breed conflict and confusion. A significant role of the U.S. Supreme Court is to settle differences in law that occur among various circuit courts.

The legal environment of affirmative action has always been murky at best, but the disparities among circuits over the past decade have significantly compounded the issue, leaving many universities to question how, if at all, to use race as a factor in admissions. Confusion and disagreement among the circuits regarding Justice Powell's opinion in *Bakke* was finally addressed when the U.S. Supreme Court undertook a review of race-conscious admissions policies in *Gratz* v. *Bollinger* and *Grutter* v. *Bollinger.*

The Michigan Cases

Each of the plaintiffs in the Michigan cases sued the University of Michigan over the use of race in admissions decisions, with *Gratz* addressing the undergraduate admissions process and *Grutter* addressing the admissions process of the university's law school. The decisions of the Court should be read together in order to determine the legal landscape of affirmative action in higher education today.

Gratz **v.** *Bollinger.* At issue in *Gratz* was a point-scale system used for undergraduate admissions to the University of Michigan. Points were awarded based on the applicant's high school grade point average, standardized test scores, high school academic quality, high school curriculum, residency, alumni relationships, personal essay, and personal achievement or leadership. Under this system, twenty points were awarded to applicants who were members of an underrepresented racial or ethnic minority group. Although Jennifer Gratz and Patrick Hamacher, each Caucasian and each Michigan residents, had point totals falling within the qualified range, both were denied admission to the College of Literature, Science, and Arts. Gratz

NEW DIRECTIONS FOR INSTITUTIONAL RESEARCH • DOI: 10.1002/ir

and Hamacher subsequently sued the university, alleging that the use of points to benefit underrepresented minorities violated both the Fourteenth Amendment and the Civil Rights Act of 1964.

The *Gratz* (2003) court concluded that Michigan's undergraduate admissions policy was "not narrowly tailored to achieve the interest in educational diversity" and therefore was unconstitutional (p. 270). The Court found significant that the Michigan point system did not individually capture what an applicant might contribute to diversity on campus, but rather arbitrarily awarded points based solely on whether the applicant was a member of an "underrepresented minority group" (pp. 271–272). The Court did not find significant, however, that the point system was developed in order to ease the administrative burden of reviewing the many applications made to the university. In other words, administrative convenience is not a justification for failing to pass a strict scrutiny review.

Grutter v. Bollinger. In *Grutter,* the sister case to *Gratz,* the issue in question was the admission policy of the Michigan Law School to individually consider each applicant's "talents, experiences, and potential 'to contribute to the learning of those around them'" (*Grutter,* 2003, p. 315). The law school considered race one type of diversity and used it in conjunction with a variety of other qualifications, including an assessment of academic ability and potential for success. The petitioner, Barbara Grutter, a Caucasian and Michigan resident, was denied admission to the law school. In her lawsuit against the university, she alleged that she was the victim of reverse discrimination because the law school used race as a "predominant" factor in its admissions decision (p. 317). The *Grutter* court, however, upheld the Michigan Law School's admissions policy. According to the record on appeal, the trial court heard the testimony of many witnesses regarding the importance of diversity to the education experience. As one witness testified, when a so-called critical mass of underrepresented students is present, "racial stereotypes lose their force because non-minority students learn there is no 'minority viewpoint' but rather a variety of viewpoints among minority students" (pp. 319–320).

The *Grutter* court ultimately endorsed Justice Powell's opinion in *Bakke* that "student body diversity is a compelling state interest that can justify the use of race in university admissions" and that such programs are subject to strict scrutiny in order to 'smoke out' illegitimate uses of race by assuring that [government] is pursuing a goal important enough to warrant use of a highly suspect tool" (pp. 325–326). With respect to the Michigan Law School specifically, the *Grutter* court stated that its decision was "informed by our view that attaining a diverse student body is at the heart of the Law School's proper institutional mission, and that 'good faith' on the part of a university is 'presumed' absent 'a showing to the contrary'" (p. 330).

Notwithstanding the *Grutter* court's conclusion, it is important to recognize that the Court did not endorse a quota system. As the Court noted, the Michigan Law School did not predetermine a critical mass of underrepresented students and subsequently seek to fill the entering class with that

NEW DIRECTIONS FOR INSTITUTIONAL RESEARCH • DOI: 10.1002/ir

number of students, as doing so "would amount to outright racial balancing, which is patently unconstitutional" (p. 330). Important to its review of the Michigan Law School's admissions system, therefore, the *Grutter* court looked to how the law school used numbers in determining critical mass. The Court, quoting Justice Powell's opinion in *Bakke,* stated that "some attention to 'numbers,' without more, does not transform a flexible admissions system into a rigid quota" (p. 336).

Subsequent Developments in the Michigan Cases

Although the Michigan cases affirmed the precedent of student body diversity as a compelling government interest, many scholars and practitioners have struggled with the implications of the Michigan cases and how to apply them in practice. Such perplexity, at least in part, led the U.S. Supreme Court to readdress affirmative action policies in its consolidated opinion in *Parents Involved in Community Schools* v. *Seattle School District No. 1* (2007) and *Meredith* v. *Jefferson County Board of Education* (2007). In *Parents* and *Meredith,* the Court addressed whether a primary public school could choose to classify students by race in order to make school assignments. The Court ultimately struck down the programs in question because they were not part of an individualized review; rather, decisions were based on race alone where race came into play (*Parents Involved in Community Schools,* p. 15). In delivering the Court's opinion, Chief Justice John Roberts went on to announce that *Grutter* did not govern *Parents* and *Meredith* because *Grutter* was meant to apply in the higher education context.

Although great caution should be observed before applying legal precedent from primary and secondary education to higher education, there are some important points to be learned from *Parents* and *Meredith.* First, the Court seemed to clarify that in order to comply with *Grutter,* institutions should make certain that applicants are considered on an individual basis rather than through a mechanical, impersonal formula. Second, Justice Roberts contended in his opinion that race may be used only in the context of a broader diversity agenda that takes into account all forms of diversity, not simply race alone.

Many supporters of affirmative action practices in higher education initially embraced the Court's rulings in *Parents* and *Meredith.* However, it is too early to tell exactly how these decisions will affect diversity initiatives in higher education. While the conservative majority of the Court led by Justice Roberts treated *Grutter* as established precedent, some commentators have argued that the rulings took a tough stance toward the traditional defenses and justifications of promoting diversity. In effect, some argue, *Parents* and *Meredith* placed additional limits on the use of race, which may well set the stage for another round of litigation. Should the Court decide to revisit the law as embodied in the *Bakke, Grutter, Gratz, Parents,* and *Meredith* decisions, the Court may add more clarification regarding whether college admissions policies are sufficient and narrowly tailored, can consider an applicant as an individual, and are part of a larger agenda of promoting diversity.

Implications and Recommendations for Practice

Five recommendations emerge for institutional researchers and other practitioners based on an analysis of the Supreme Court's ruling in *Gratz* and *Grutter*. We echo Luna's concern (2006) regarding the difficulty in making decisions and policies from individual court cases that are heavily influenced by the particular facts of the case at hand. There are some specific standards that the Court has identified as areas that need to be addressed by colleges and universities. We use these standards to form recommendations for practice:

1. *Conduct a periodic review of existing affirmative action policies and the need for such policies.* Writing for the majority in *Grutter*, Justice Sandra Day O'Connor opined that the need for affirmative action may be unnecessary in twenty-five years. The addition of a time limit as part of the test for narrowly tailoring a race-conscious admissions program posits that the need for affirmative action is temporary and needed to fulfill the goal of equality only in the short term. As such, when race-conscious admissions policies are no longer needed to foster student diversity, the institution should discontinue them. In *Grutter*, the Court mandated review but did not specify a time frame for periodic reviews. As part of this review, universities should examine race-neutral policy options and evaluate whether these options alone can fulfill the institution's need for a diverse student body. A significant aspect of the review should examine admissions goals and processes, ensuring the two are directly linked. The university should assess the types of diversity sought and the goals for achieving these ends. The evaluation and assessment of diversity should keep in mind the mission of the university and how diversity helps the university accomplish its mission. Periodic reviews of the kind we describe here will ensure that affirmative action policies further the educational objectives of the university, are narrowly tailored and necessary, and are effectively meeting the stated admissions and diversity goals of the institution.

2. *Document the link between racial diversity and the mission of the institution.* As part of its defense in the *Gratz* and *Grutter* cases, the University of Michigan provided a wealth of empirical support for the educational benefits of diversity in higher education. These types of data demonstrate the depth and sound judgment of the institution in deciding to make use of race and ethnicity as a factor in admissions decisions. Institutional researchers and other university administrators should systematically collect data to support the benefits of diversity in fulfilling the mission of the university. In the event of future affirmative

action litigation, extensive data supporting the use of racial criteria provide the courts with a rationale for the use of race, including its pivotal role in attaining educational outcomes. Universities that document how diversity improves their campuses both inside and outside the classroom will be best positioned to make the argument for the compelling interest of diversity. Longitudinal approaches can provide a history of lessons learned and changes made to race-conscious policies that can demonstrate the institution's efforts to conform to the narrow tailoring required by the courts.

3. *Build a strong database of evidence of the effects of past discrimination.* Although much of the discussion in this chapter has focused on the educational benefits of diversity, the U.S. Supreme Court has found that the continuing effects of past institutional discrimination can be a compelling interest in justifying affirmative action policies. An institution seeking to use this rationale to substantiate the use of race-conscious policies should develop a robust evidentiary basis to support this argument. Due to the significant threshold that must be reached in order to successfully argue the need for remedial policies, remedial policies must be considerably supported by institutional evidence. This evidence can include the statistical disparity in minority attendance, for example, but also should include qualitative data to provide needed depth to the numerical evidence. Such qualitative information could provide a court with a fuller explanation that past discrimination is the cause of the current statistical differences at the institution.

4. *Examine the effects of admissions policies that give preference to legacies.* For universities that give preferential admissions treatment to the relatives of alumni, institutional researchers need to examine the effects of legacy policies on the diversity of the student body. Allocating admissions spots for legacies who are more likely to be both majority and wealthy can limit the goal of increasing diversity. The argument that affirmative action is needed to promote diversity when the institution regularly sets aside seats in the class is untenable at best. Understanding the effect of these policies is important for universities in setting a comprehensive enrollment management strategy that will withstand the scrutiny of the courts.

5. *Do not set quotas or otherwise directly rely on statistical data when making admissions decisions.* Although race-conscious admissions policies are permissible if narrowly tailored, quotas and set-asides, whether explicit or implicit, are clearly impermissible. Accordingly, admissions officers should not review statistics regarding the racial composition of an entering class during the admissions process, because doing so may tarnish the admissions process and result in the inadvertent creation of a quota or set-aside. In order to avoid any chance or appearance of impropriety, such statistics should be maintained by another unit of the

university and, subsequent to the closing of admissions for a particular academic year, analyzed to assess the effectiveness of the race-conscious admissions policy.

Conclusion

Until the U.S. Supreme Court reconsiders its decisions in *Gratz* and *Grutter,* higher education will be permitted to use race as a factor in college admissions decisions. The exception to using race as a factor is the increased use of the statewide referendum by opponents of affirmative action to ban the use of race. Although institutions have limited control over the referendum process, the systematic collection and dissemination of the benefits of diversity can make a stronger case for the need of diversity in higher education. Colleges and universities should not believe that the constitutionality of race-conscious admissions is settled law, never again to be readdressed. The increased conservative majority of the U.S. Supreme Court following the retirement of Justice Sandra Day O'Connor and the appointment of Chief Justice John Roberts and Justice Samuel Alito only increases the imperative for higher education to document the need for, and benefit of, student diversity. Justice O'Connor herself left open the door for an eventual reexamination of the need for affirmative action admissions programs. The increased participation of minorities since the *Brown v. Board of Education* decision over fifty years ago has been a positive outcome for higher education. However, more assimilation is needed to fully integrate and involve minority students. The collection of comprehensive and robust data to support the goals of affirmative action will likely be a significant aspect of the next landmark affirmative action case in higher education twenty or thirty years from today.

References

Bowen, W., and Bok, D. *The Shape of the River: Long-Term Consequences of Considering Race in College and University Admissions.* Princeton, N.J.: Princeton University Press, 1998.

Chang, M. "Does Diversity Matter? The Educational Impact of a Racially Diverse Undergraduate Population." *Journal of College Student Development,* 1999, 40(4), 377–395.

Chang, M. "The Impact of an Undergraduate Diversity Course Requirement on Students' Racial Views and Attitudes." *Journal of General Education,* 2002, 51(1), 22–42.

Gratz v. Bollinger, 539 U.S. 244 (2003).

Grutter v. Bollinger, 539 U.S. 306 (2003).

Gurin, P. "Expert Report of Patricia Gurin in the Case of *Gratz, et al.* v. *Bollinger, et al.,* No. 97–75321 and *Grutter, et al.* v. *Bollinger, et al.,* No. 97–75928." Retrieved June 25, 2007, from http://www.vpcomm.umich.edu/admissions/legal/expert/gurintoc.html, 1999.

Gurin, P., Dey, E., Hurtado, S., and Gurin, G. "Diversity and Higher Education: Theory and Impact on Educational Outcomes." *Harvard Educational Review,* 2002, 72(3), 330–366.

Hopwood v. Texas, 78 F.3d 932 (1996).

Kaplin, W., and Lee, B. *The Law of Higher Education.* San Francisco: Jossey-Bass, 2006.

Luna, A. "Faculty Salary Equity Cases: Combining Statistics with the Law." *Journal of Higher Education,* 2006, 77(2), 193–224.

Meredith v. Jefferson County Board of Education, 551 U.S. (2007).

Milem, J. "The Educational Benefits of Diversity: Evidence from Multiple Sectors." In M. Chang, D. Witt, J. Jones, and K. Hakuta (eds.), *Compelling Interest: Examining the Evidence on Racial Dynamics in Colleges and Universities.* Stanford, Calif.: Stanford University Press, 2003.

Parents Involved in Community Schools v. Seattle School District No. 1, 551 U.S. (2007).

Pascarella, E., and Terenzini, P. *How College Affects Students.* San Francisco: Jossey-Bass, 1991.

Piaget, J. *The Moral Judgment of the Child.* New York: Free Press, 1965.

Regents of the University of California v. Bakke, 438 U.S. 265 (1978).

Smith v. University of Washington Law School, 233 F.3d 1188 (2000).

Terenzini, P., and others. "Racial and Ethnic Diversity in the Classroom: Does It Promote Student Learning?" *Journal of Higher Education,* 2001, 72(5), 509–531.

Whitt, E., and others. "Influences on Student's Openness to Diversity and Challenge in the Second and Third Years of College." *Journal of Higher Education,* 2001, 72(2), 172–204.

MICHAEL S. HARRIS is an assistant professor of higher education at the University of Alabama.

JOHN H. ROTH is an attorney in private practice.

This chapter examines the statistical evidence used to determine whether an institution's athletic program is in compliance with Title IX.

Statistical Evidence and Compliance with Title IX

John J. Cheslock, Suzanne E. Eckes

The thirty-fifth anniversary of Title IX was observed in 2007. This landmark legislation states in part, "No person in the United States shall, on the basis of sex, be excluded from participation in, be denied the benefits of, or be subjected to discrimination under any educational program or activity receiving federal financial assistance" (from the Preamble to Title IX). The scope of Title IX clearly includes all aspects of education, but the legislation's application to college athletics receives the most attention. Athletics programs, unlike most academic activities, are sex segregated, so the proper interpretation of the intercollegiate athletics provisions of Title IX is less clear-cut.

In this chapter, we outline the interpretation of Title IX that has developed over the past thirty-five years. We review the original 1979 policy interpretation as well as the 1996 and 2005 policy clarifications produced by the Office for Civil Rights (OCR). We also review the case law for Title IX, highlighting a number of key court decisions that altered the seriousness with which institutions considered this law when planning their athletic programs. This chapter also includes an examination of the current level of compliance with the intercollegiate athletic participation requirements of Title IX.

Throughout the chapter, we highlight issues of relevance to institutional researchers. The OCR policy interpretation and clarifications provide clear statements about the proper data to use to demonstrate compliance

NEW DIRECTIONS FOR INSTITUTIONAL RESEARCH, no. 138, Summer 2008 © Wiley Periodicals, Inc.
Published online in Wiley InterScience (www.interscience.wiley.com) • DOI: 10.1002/ir.246

under Title IX, and court rulings typically use these measurements. We identify the exact data that institutions need to provide to demonstrate compliance and devote one section of the chapter to outlining some of the mistakes institutional researchers commonly make when reporting these data. As a result of the Equity in Athletics Disclosure Act (EADA), all higher education institutions must annually report data documenting their level of gender equity in intercollegiate athletics.

Policy Interpretation and Clarifications

The interpretation of Title IX's application to intercollegiate athletics was a complicated and drawn-out process. The initial regulations, first published in 1975, produced numerous complaints, and a 1978 draft policy interpretation that contained substantial revisions also drew opposition. The final interpretation, published in 1979, differed substantially from the earlier attempts and became an important guide for colleges and universities seeking to demonstrate compliance under Title IX. In fact, Suggs (2005) states that "the 1979 interpretation is, from a legal standpoint, the most influential document issued to explain how gender equity should work in college sports" (p. 78).

The 1979 policy interpretation notes schools' obligations in three areas: athletic financial assistance (scholarships), other athletic benefits and opportunities, and the effective accommodation of student interests and abilities through the provision of participation opportunities. The scholarship section is straightforward. An institution may be found in compliance if the female share of athletes is substantially equal to the female share of athletic financial aid. So if 45 percent of an institution's athletes are female, close to 45 percent of the financial aid must be provided to women. The policy interpretation notes that small differences in these two figures are allowed, but the specific size at which they become substantially unequal is not specified. Even if an institution has disparities in its female share of athletes and female share of aid, it can demonstrate compliance by noting legitimate nondiscriminatory factors that explain the disparity. A nondiscriminatory difference in the share of out-of-state scholarships for men and women at public institutions is an example of a legitimate factor.

Relative to the other two areas, the part of the policy interpretation covering other athletic benefits and opportunities is vague and lengthy. This section includes a long list of program components, mentioning such areas as publicity, recruitment, support services, equipment, supplies, travel, per diem expenses, locker rooms, practice facilities, and the opportunity to receive coaching and academic tutoring. The interpretation does allow the OCR director to consider program components beyond those that are listed, so the potential scope of this section is immense.

No specific guidelines for determining compliance with any of the program components are provided. The policy interpretation does provide some general considerations and lists a number of specific factors to consider for each component. A reading of these factors suggests that a meaningful demonstration of full compliance for each program component would require a thorough and expensive audit. For example, equivalence in equipment and supplies, one of the eleven components listed, requires equivalence in quality, amount, suitability, maintenance, replacement, and availability.

To determine whether a higher education institution is effectively accommodating the interests and ability of its students, the policy interpretation outlines a three-part test (U.S. Department of Education, 1997):

Prong One: Substantial Proportionality. This part of the test is satisfied when participation opportunities for men and women are "substantially proportionate" to their respective undergraduate enrollments.

Prong Two: History and Continuing Practice. This part of the test is satisfied when an institution has a history and continuing practice of program expansion that is responsive to the developing interests and abilities of the underrepresented sex (typically female).

Prong Three: Effectively Accommodating Interests and Abilities. This part of the test is satisfied when an institution is meeting the interests and abilities of its female students even where there are disproportionately fewer females than males participating in sports.

An institution is in compliance with the first prong when its female share of athletes is approximately equal to its female share of undergraduates. So if women comprise 53 percent of an institution's student body, women should also comprise approximately 53 percent of its athletes. The original policy interpretation does not specify how different these two figures can become before they are no longer substantially proportionate. The policy interpretation also provides little guidance regarding the evidence needed to demonstrate compliance with the second and third prongs.

The next section demonstrates that several key judicial decisions caused the seriousness with which colleges and universities considered Title IX to increase steadily in the 1990s. The decisions also suggested that the three-part test for effective accommodation of interests and abilities has "become the key to judicial evaluation of compliance with Title IX's athletic regulations" (Johnson, 1994, p. 580). As a result, the policy interpretation came under increasing scrutiny, especially the section regarding the third prong. Two complaints emerged. First, many colleges and universities did not feel they had sufficient information to determine whether they were in compliance under the three-prong test. In addition, critics argued that the OCR relied too heavily on the first prong (substantial proportionality) and wanted clear evidence that institutions could comply with the latter two prongs.

The OCR responded by issuing a policy clarification in 1996 that provided additional guidance for all three prongs. For the first prong, this clarification noted that substantial proportionality is achieved "when the number of opportunities that would be required to achieve proportionality would not be sufficient to sustain a viable team" (OCR, 1996, p. 5). The clarification also noted that schools could use natural fluctuations in undergraduate enrollment to explain slight departures from substantial proportionality.

For the second prong, the OCR noted that there are no fixed intervals of time or number of added teams that automatically demonstrate that an institution has a history and continuing practice of program expansion for the underrepresented gender. Instead, an institution must demonstrate that the "program expansion was responsive to developing interests and abilities of the underrepresented sex" (OCR, 1996, p. 6). The policy clarification then provides general descriptions of the evidence that can be used to demonstrate compliance under the second prong and several examples of institutions in and out of compliance.

The OCR notes that compliance under the third prong cannot occur when, for the underrepresented gender, there is sufficient interest to support an intercollegiate team, sufficient ability to sustain the intercollegiate team, and reasonable expectation of competition for the team. The policy clarification outlines the numerous pieces of data that the OCR will collect and analyze to determine whether all three requirements for noncompliance are met. No specific criteria for analyzing the data are included, although the policy implication does note that an institution may assess athletic interest "using nondiscriminatory methods of its choosing" (OCR, 1996, p. 8).

A 2005 policy clarification provided much more specificity regarding the third prong by outlining a Web-based prototype survey that "institutions can rely on as an acceptable method to measure students' interest in participating in sports" (OCR, 2005, p. 2). The clarification was accompanied by a user's guide and a detailed technical report that describes this survey, which must be administered to all full-time undergraduate students of the underrepresented sex. Unless the OCR "finds direct and very persuasive evidence of unmet interest sufficient to sustain a varsity team, such as the recent elimination of a viable team for the underrepresented gender or a recent, broad-based petition from an existing club team for elevation to varsity status," an institution will be in compliance with the third prong if the model survey shows insufficient interest to field a varsity team (OCR, 2005, p. 2). This 2005 clarification differed fundamentally from the 1996 clarification because the earlier document stated that the OCR would use a broader set of information, including participation data from regional high schools and amateur athletic associations, in its determination of compliance.

The model survey suggested by the OCR has met with some resistance. Supporters of previous Title IX interpretations have raised questions about the methodology underlying it (Sabo and Grant, 2005). The leadership of the National Collegiate Athletic Association (2005) also expressed concern and recommended that its members not use the procedures outlined in the 2005 clarification.

The 1996 and 2005 policy clarifications did not just differ in their criteria for compliance with the third prong: they also differed substantially in tone. The 1996 clarification notes that substantial proportionality provides institutions with a safe harbor, but institutions can still demonstrate compliance through the second and third prongs. In contrast, the 2005 clarification notes that all three prongs are safe harbors and that the burden of proof is on the OCR or on students (if a complaint is filed) to "show by a preponderance of the evidence that the institution is not in compliance with prong three" (OCR, 2005, p. 2). These differences in tone reflect the different administrations in place at the time of the two clarifications.

The administration appointing the OCR leadership can also influence the level of enforcement of Title IX. The original 1979 policy interpretation outlined that the OCR needed to periodically conduct compliance reviews for a number of institutions and investigate all valid complaints alleging discrimination on the basis of gender. The OCR was relatively passive in its enforcement of Title IX until appointees from the Clinton administration increased enforcement (Suggs, 2005). These efforts may not have carried over to the more recent Bush administration. A recent review found that between 2002 and 2006, the OCR conducted only one compliance review that focused on whether a higher education institution's athletics department met with Title IX's substantive requirements (National Women's Law Center, 2007). Most of the compliance reviews conducted by the OCR simply examined institutions' Title IX grievance procedures and sexual harassment policies.

Selected Title IX Court Cases: How the Courts Have Measured Compliance

Some observers have argued that litigation is the most effective avenue to ensure that universities comply with Title IX. This section highlights several of the key Title IX cases in higher education. (For additional information on Title IX litigation, see Eckes, 2003, 2004.) These cases have helped decipher the statutory maze of Title IX and have provided universities with clearer guidelines regarding what constitutes compliance. At issue in the lawsuits is the interpretation of the three-part test, as well as how much deference should be given to the Department of Education's interpretation of the 1975 regulations embodied within the 1979 policy interpretation (Harris, 1994; Stevens, 2004).

In order to establish a prima facie Title IX case, the plaintiff has the burden to prove the following: (1) an educational program is involved, (2) the defendant entity is the recipient of federal funds, and (3) discrimination occurred on the basis of sex in the provision or nonprovision of the educational programs (Title IX, 1972). In examining the three-part test, eight federal circuits have upheld Title IX, its regulations, and the 1979 policy interpretation. It is also important to note that as a result of the U.S. Supreme Court's decision in *Franklin v. Gwinnett County Public Schools* (1992), plaintiffs can recover monetary damages for violations of Title IX. This decision broadened Title IX's enforcement by allowing a damages remedy.

NEW DIRECTIONS FOR INSTITUTIONAL RESEARCH • DOI: 10.1002/ir

Both males and females have initiated the lawsuits in the key Title IX cases examined in this chapter. Often female athletes argue that the university should reinstate or create a women's varsity athletic team. In contrast, male athletes often allege reverse discrimination under Title IX when a men's athletic team is cut or demoted. Both male-initiated and female-initiated cases demonstrate the analytical puzzles posed by Title IX (Lamber, 2000).

One of the most significant Title IX cases was *Cohen v. Brown University* (1996). In *Cohen,* the First Circuit Court of Appeals relied heavily on the first prong of the policy interpretation's three-part test to determine compliance. In so doing, the court held that the university failed the effective accommodation test (*Cohen v. Brown University,* 1993). In this case, due to budget cuts, the university demoted men's varsity golf and water polo and women's varsity gymnastics and volleyball from university-funded status to donor-funded status. As a result, females from the gymnastics and volleyball teams filed a lawsuit (*Cohen v. Brown University,* 1992). In addition to prohibiting the university from eliminating any other female teams "unless the percentage of opportunities to participate in intercollegiate athletics equals the percentage of women enrolled in the undergraduate program" (prong one) (*Cohen v. Brown University,* 1992, p. 980), the female athletes contended that the women's gymnastics and volleyball teams should be reinstated to varsity status. The female athletes also argued that the interests and abilities compliance area (prong three) of Title IX had been violated by the university.

To demonstrate compliance with Title IX, Brown University needed to satisfy the requirements of one of the three prongs. In applying the three-part test, the court found that the university failed to meet the requirements of the first prong because the student body population and athletic composition were not substantially proportionate. According to the court, the university failed to fulfill the second prong because it did not continue to expand the women's athletic programs in the 1980s and 1990s. When applying the third prong, the court found that there was enough female interest and ability to support the gymnastics and volleyball teams. As such, the First Circuit affirmed the district court's opinion and reinstated the women's gymnastics and volleyball teams (*Cohen v. Brown University,* 1993). Significantly, the court reasoned that the appropriate standard in achieving substantial proportionality (prong one) is related to the number of participants on male and female teams, not the amount of money spent on each team. Importantly, the court noted that the first prong provides "a safe harbor for those institutions that have distributed athletic opportunities in numbers 'substantially proportionate' to the gender composition of their student bodies" (*Cohen v. Brown University,* 1993, p. 897).

The First Circuit heard this case again in 1996 after it had been remanded back to the district court. In the 1996 case, Brown University contended that "an athletics program equally accommodates both genders and complies with Title IX if it accommodates the relative interests and abilities of its male and female students" (*Cohen* v. *University,* 1996, p. 174). The court rejected the university's argument—that males were more interested in athletics than females—because it relied on false stereotypes. In so doing, the court dismissed statistical evidence demonstrating the level of interest in female athletics because these findings were "only a measure of the very discrimination that is and has been the basis for women's lack of opportunity to participate in sports" (pp. 179–180). Again, the court placed significance on the first prong and interpreted "substantial proportionality" to mean "gender balance of its intercollegiate athletic program substantially mirrors the gender balance of its student enrollment" (p. 200).

The parties settled the case in 1998 and, with court approval, the university agreed to provide athletic opportunities for females in close proportion (within 3.5 percent) to the percentage of female students enrolled. This decision was especially important because it helped shape and define the standard for Title IX compliance when using the three-part test (Stevens, 2004). Almost every circuit court that has reviewed a Title IX discrimination claim in intercollegiate athletics has followed *Cohen's* analysis of the regulation and policy interpretation.

Similarly, the Third Circuit Court of Appeals held in *Favia* v. *Indiana University of Pennsylvania* (1993b) (referred to as *Favia II*) that the university failed to demonstrate that it met any of the requirements of the three-part test. This case was filed after the Indiana University of Pennsylvania cut the women's gymnastics and field hockey teams. The district court found that the discrepancy between female and male participation was problematic and that the continuing expansion, under prong two, had not been met because the number of women's teams at the university had decreased. The university also failed to meet the compliance requirements under prong three because the court found notable female interest in gymnastics and field hockey (*Favia* v. *Indiana University of Pennsylvania,* 1993a). The district court also denied the university's "financial hardship defense" (p. 585). The Third Circuit affirmed the district court's decision finding that the university did not provide equal opportunities for female athletes (*Favia* v. *Indiana University of Pennsylvania,* 1993b). The Third Circuit noted that the 17.8 percent discrepancy between the percentage of female students enrolled at the university and female athletes was too great a difference to be considered substantially proportionate under prong one.

The Tenth Circuit Court of Appeals found in *Roberts* v. *Colorado State Board of Agriculture* (1993b) that the university had not provided effective accommodation to female athletes. Like *Cohen* and *Favia,* the *Roberts* decision also helped set the standard for interpreting the three-part test (Alacbay, 2004). In this case, Colorado State University dropped its women's varsity softball team, and the female athletes argued that the decision to terminate the team violated Title IX because there was no effective accommodation of the interests and abilities of the underrepresented gender. The university contended that there was no Title IX violation because the men's baseball team had also been eliminated. The district court disagreed and ordered the university to reinstate the softball team to varsity status (*Roberts* v. *Colorado State University,* 1993a). Upholding the reinstatement of the teams, the Tenth Circuit found that the university did not comply with any of the three prongs of the three-part test (*Roberts* v. *Colorado State University,* 1993a).

When analyzing prong one, the court observed that the enrollment discrepancy between females and males was similar to what occurred in *Cohen.* The court found a 10.5 percent difference between female students enrolled at Colorado State University and female athletes. The court also stated that "financially strapped institutions may still comply with Title IX by cutting athletic programs such that men's and women's athletic participation rates become substantially proportionate to their representation in the undergraduate population" (p. 830). Regarding prong two, the court found that the university did not adequately expand sports programs for women. In examining prong three, the court reasoned that the university is permitted to discontinue the underrepresented gender's team only when "there is no reasonable expectation of competition for that team within the institution's normal competitive region" (*Roberts* v. *Colorado State University,* 1993a, p. 831). The courts' similar interpretations of Title IX in *Cohen, Favia,* and *Roberts* were given further support when the Supreme Court denied certiorari in *Roberts* (Eckes, 2004).

In another female-initiated lawsuit, the Fifth Circuit Court of Appeals measured compliance differently in *Pederson* v. *Louisiana State University* (2000). In this case, female students initiated a lawsuit alleging that the university violated Title IX by not supporting a female varsity soccer and softball team. This case was different from the earlier ones because the lawsuit was initiated by females who had never participated in the varsity athletic program; they wanted the university to create two new teams.

Although the court did find that Louisiana State University violated Title IX, it did not apply the three-part test in the same way that *Cohen* and the other courts have done. Specifically, the district court did not use numerical percentages in the same manner (*Pederson* v. *Louisiana State University,* 1996). As noted in *Cohen,* the court had focused on prong one (substantial proportionality). In *Pederson,* the court rejected the reliance on the substantial proportionality prong and argued that under *Cohen,* a court must assume that the interest and ability to participate in sports is equal between males and females. In *Pederson,* the court rejected this argument and did not find that there would be the same levels of interest for males and females at all universities. No other federal courts have fully adopted the analysis of the *Pederson* decision.

In addition to women bringing Title IX lawsuits, men have also tried to make headway in court, often claiming violations of both Title IX and the equal protection clause of the Fourteenth Amendment (Eckes, 2004). In these cases, the courts have generally afforded deference to the U.S. Department of Education's interpretation of the 1975 regulations embodied within the 1979 policy interpretation. In so doing, the courts have fairly consistently rejected the men's claims.

Kelley v. *Board of Trustees* (1994) was one of the first important male-initiated lawsuits. In *Kelley,* male team members at the University of Illinois alleged reverse discrimination because the demotion of their teams violated Title IX. In this case, the university eliminated the men's swimming, fencing, and diving teams and the women's diving team because of budget constraints. The Seventh Circuit found that the participation ratios were substantially disproportionate to the student body because females occupied only 23 percent of the intercollegiate participation slots in comparison to the 44 percent female student body (*Kelley* v. *Board of Trustees,* 1994). The male team members argued that prong one of the three-part test created an artificial quota. The court denied this claim and stated:

> The policy interpretation does not, as plaintiffs suggest, mandate statistical balancing. Rather the policy interpretation merely creates a presumption that a school is in compliance with Title IX and the applicable regulation when it achieves such a statistical balance. Even if substantial proportionality has not been achieved, a school may establish that it is in compliance by demonstrating either that it has a continuing practice of increasing the athletic opportunities of the underrepresented sex or that its existing programs effectively accommodate the interests of that sex [*Kelley* v. *Board of Trustees,* 1994, p. 271].

Relying on the holding in *Cohen,* the court reasoned that the decision to cut the men's team was a "reasonable response" to the Title IX regulations (p. 270). It permitted the University of Illinois to eliminate the men's swim team while maintaining the women's swim team because male athletes "would continue to be more substantially proportionate to their presence in the University's student body" (p. 270).

In *Boulahanis* v. *Board of Regents of Illinois State University* (1999), the university eliminated the men's wrestling and soccer teams in order to meet Title IX's statutory requirements. The male athletes filed a lawsuit alleging a Title IX violation because their teams were purposefully eliminated to make additional opportunities for women. The female students also alleged discrimination based on the elimination of the men's athletic teams in lieu of adding more female teams. The court dismissed the female students' claims because they did not have standing. Standing requires that a plaintiff demonstrate that he or she was harmed by the law. In this case, the court did not find that the female plaintiffs had suffered any injuries when additional female teams were not added. The district court granted the university's motion for summary judgment (see *Harper* v. *Board of Regents of Illinois State University,* 1999). The Seventh Circuit affirmed finding that it was permissible for the university to eliminate the teams in order to meet the requirements of Title IX. Specifically, the court found that the university's elimination of men's wrestling and soccer was "not a violation of Title IX as long as men's participation in athletics continues to be 'substantially proportionate' to their enrollment" (*Boulahanis* v. *Board of Regents of Illinois State University,* 1999, p. 638).

Similarly, in *Neal* v. *Board of Trustees of the California State Universities* (1999), a wrestling program was downsized, and the male athletes alleged that the university had violated Title IX. The district court relied on the *Pederson* decision in finding that "the *Pederson* court's rejection of the safe harbor test is sensible. This court essentially finds that the safe harbor rule is not dictated by the Policy Interpretation and is inconsistent with the text, structure and policy of the Title IX itself" (*Neal* v. *Board of Trustees of California State University,* 1997, p. 12). The Ninth Circuit Court of Appeals rejected this decision, holding that Title IX does not prohibit universities from taking measures that would ensure that female athletes are approximately as well represented in athletic programs as they are in student bodies. The Ninth Circuit stated, "We adopt the reasoning of *Cohen I, Cohen II,* and *Kelley,* and hold that the constitutional analysis contained therein persuasively disposes of any serious constitutional concerns that might be raised in relation to the OCR Policy Interpretation" (p. 772).

The Sixth and Eighth Circuit Courts of Appeals addressed similar legal issues initiated in court by male athletes. In *Miami University Wrestling Club* v. *Miami University* (2002), the male athletes alleged that the university's elimination of the men's wrestling, tennis, and soccer teams constituted gender discrimination under Title IX. Within their complaint, they contended that the 1979 policy interpretation is not entitled to deference but that even if it is entitled to some deference, it is not a persuasive interpretation of Title IX (Eckes, 2004). Relying on precedent, the court found that the policy interpretation is entitled to deference and is entitled to "controlling weight" (p. 615). The Sixth Circuit Court of Appeals affirmed the district court's summary judgment motion and dismissed the male athletes' action (*Miami University Wrestling Club* v. *Miami University,* 2002). A motion for summary judgment is used by parties in a lawsuit to have a case dismissed by the judge before it moves to trial. When granting a motion for summary judgment, the moving party needs to demonstrate that no issue of material fact exists and that the lawsuit should be dismissed.

Also, in *Chalenor* v. *University of North Dakota* (2002), the Eighth Circuit Court of Appeals upheld the three-part test when it ruled in favor of the university. In this case, the court examined whether Title IX prohibits a public university from eliminating a male athletic team for the purpose of reducing the inequality of athletic participation between male and female students. The members of the wrestling team argued that eliminating the men's wrestling team was gender discrimination under Title IX. The University of North Dakota argued that it was facing budget constraints and that a greater percentage of men than women at the university participated in intercollegiate athletics. The university also asserted that men received a disproportionately large share of the athletic budget; therefore, continuing to fund the team would have violated Title IX.

Furthermore, members of the wrestling team believed that budgetary matters should not have been a factor because a private donor had offered to fund the wrestling program. The wrestling team members also alleged that the district court's decision was analogous to implementing a quota system and that the University of North Dakota was improperly assuming that men and women have an equal interest in participating in university sports. In making these arguments, the male athletes asserted that the 1996 clarification was not controlling because it was only an advisory letter.

In response to the private donor issue, the court found that "a public university cannot avoid its legal obligations by substituting funds from private sources for funds from tax revenues" (*Chalenor* v. *University of North Dakota*, 2002, p. 1048). Specifically, when a university receives privately donated money, it is considered public money and therefore subject to Title IX compliance. Regarding the quota system argument, the court found that the university properly understood that gender proportionality is not required, only that it is permissible. The court also relied on the decisions of other circuit courts holding that a university may bring itself into Title IX compliance by increasing opportunities for the underrepresented gender or reducing opportunities for the overrepresented gender. In so doing, the court stated: "We conclude as did the [*Brown*] court, that the policy interpretation constitutes a reasonable and 'considered interpretation of the regulation.' Therefore controlling deference is due it" (*Chalenor* v. *University of North Dakota*, 2002, p. 1047).

The male-initiated cases have remained consistent with the precedent established in *Kelley* and *Cohen* and provide guidance regarding what federal courts found to be acceptable ways to satisfy compliance under Title IX. Furthermore, the compliance cases serve as a rough guideline as to what may numerically constitute substantial proportionality. More important, the cases demonstrate that the standard is somewhat flexible and that there is some variance among the courts (Stevens, 2004).

Equity in Athletics Disclosure Act

In 1994, Congress passed the Equity in Athletics Disclosure Act (EADA), which requires higher education institutions to disclose extensive data on their athletic program to the public. When the EADA took effect for the 1995–1996 academic year, schools were required to disclose this information only in response to specific requests by members of the public. Congress later adjusted the EADA so that starting in 2000–2001, higher education institutions were required to send these data to the Office of Postsecondary Education, which then distributed this information through its Web site (http://ope.ed.gov/athletics/). Under the EADA, schools must report the numbers of participants and coaches for each sport, as well as the overall expenditures. In addition, they must outline the share of financial aid expenditures, recruiting expenditures, and operating expenses that go to female athletes.

When reporting EADA data, many colleges and universities make one error that can lead to incorrect assessments of their compliance with several requirements of Title IX: reporting of duplicated and unduplicated participation figures, which differ in their treatment of multisport athletes. Consider an athlete who participates in cross-country, indoor track and field, and outdoor track and field, the three sports on which multisport athletes usually reside. This athlete would be counted three times for the duplicated count of participants but only one time for the unduplicated count of participants.

When reporting participation figures under the EADA, the data entrant should report the duplicated count of participants unless the form specifically requests a total count of unduplicated participants. The instructions for the EADA form clearly state this, but a substantial share of institutions incorrectly report unduplicated figures. These mistakes almost always occur for cross country/track and field sports, because these sports contain the most multisport athletes and the EADA form allows an institution to report data for these sports as a group. (Schools must report data separately for all other sports.)

To demonstrate the magnitude of this mistake, consider a school that has forty-two students who participate in cross country, indoor track and field, and outdoor track and field. The roster size for cross country is fifteen, and the roster size for both indoor track and field and outdoor track and field is forty-two. In other words, fifteen athletes participate in three sports, and twenty-seven participate in two. In this case, the unduplicated count of participants for these three sports is forty-two, while the duplicated count of participants is ninety-nine. Incorrect reporting in this case can cause the institution's estimate of participants to be off by fifty-seven athletes.

An institution's compliance with the Title IX requirements should be evaluated using the unduplicated count of participants for the financial aid requirements and the duplicated count of participants for the participation requirements. If the wrong measure is used, the resulting figures can provide a misleading portrait of the institution's level of compliance. For example, most institutions overestimate their distance from meeting the substantial proportionality prong when they incorrectly report unduplicated figures (Anderson, Cheslock, and Ehrenberg, 2006).

An institution's substantial proportionality estimate will also be incorrect when it misreports its female share of undergraduates. When calculating this share, an institution should count only full-time undergraduates, but many schools incorrectly use total undergraduate enrollment figures, which also include part-time students. Because females compose a larger share of part-time undergraduates than full-time undergraduates, this mistake makes it harder for schools to meet substantial proportionality. According to Integrated Postsecondary Education Data System (IPEDS) data, the

NEW DIRECTIONS FOR INSTITUTIONAL RESEARCH • DOI: 10.1002/ir

average higher education institution with an athletic program has a female share of full-time undergraduates of 55.8 percent; the figure rises to 57.2 percent when part-time students are included in the computation.

An institutional researcher may be tempted to test for statistical significance when examining whether an institution's participation figures are substantially proportionate. The 1996 clarification, however, suggests that such a test may not be appropriate because it states that a team can be X athletes away from substantial proportionality if X athletes are not sufficient to sustain a viable team. If a difference of X athletes causes an institution's participation levels to differ from substantial proportionality in a statistically significant manner, an institution can be in compliance with the first prong of Title IX's participation requirements even if a statistical significance test suggests otherwise.

Current Levels of Compliance

Cheslock (2007) demonstrates that a majority of institutions would not meet either of the first two prongs of the three-prong test. In 2004–2005 for the 1,895 institutions studied, the average female share of undergraduates was 55.8 percent and the average female share of athletes was 41.7 percent, meaning that most institutions faced a proportionality gap of 14.1 percentage points. Eighty-seven percent of institutions had a proportionality gap above three percentage points, meaning that very few institutions can rely on the first prong to demonstrate compliance with Title IX's participation requirements.

Among those same institutions, around 26 percent added a women's team on net between 2001–2002 and 2004–2005 (Cheslock, 2007). The OCR has not outlined specific guidelines for determining compliance with the second prong, but in a 1996 policy clarification, it did provide examples of institutions that met and did not meet this prong's requirements. Nothing in that policy clarification suggests that institutions could demonstrate a history and continuing practice of program expansion when it has not added a team in the previous four years.

Conclusion

The figures suggest that most institutions must rely on the third prong to demonstrate compliance with Title IX's participation requirements. This fact is unlikely to change in the short term. Although institutions did move closer to substantial proportionality during the 1990s, this progress has slowed considerably in recent years (Anderson, Cheslock, and Ehrenberg, 2006; Cheslock, 2007).

The 2008 presidential election may drastically alter the consequences of noncompliance with the first and second prongs. Two changes are possible when new leadership takes control of the White House. The OCR's level of enforcement may increase, with a greater number of compliance reviews that focus on whether an institution's athletics department meets Title IX's substantive requirements. The OCR may also use different criteria when determining compliance with the third prong. Given the controversy surrounding the survey methods outlined in the 2005 policy clarification, this clarification may be rescinded.

References

Alacbay, A. "Are Intercollegiate Sports Programs a Buck Short? Examining the Latest Attack of Title IX." *George Mason University Civil Rights Law Journal,* 2004, *14*(2), 255–290.

Anderson, D., Cheslock, J., and Ehrenberg, R. "Gender Equity in Intercollegiate Athletics: Determinants of Title IX Compliance." *Journal of Higher Education,* 2006, *77*(2), 225–250.

Boulahanis v. Board of Regents of Illinois State University, 198 F.3d 633 (7th Cir. 1999).

Chalenor v. University of North Dakota, 291 F.3d 1042 (8th Cir. 2002).

Cheslock, J. *Who's Playing College Sports? Trends in Participation.* East Meadow, N.Y.: Women's Sports Foundation, 2007.

Cohen v. Brown University, 809 F. Supp. 978 (D.R.I. 1992).

Cohen v. Brown University, 991 F.2d 888 (1st Cir. 1993).

Cohen v. Brown University, 101 F.3d 155 (1st Cir. 1996).

Eckes, S. "The 30th Anniversary of Title IX: Women Have Not Reached the Finish Line." *University of Southern California Law Review for Women,* 2003, *13*(1), 101–132.

Eckes, S. "Another Pin for Women: The National Wrestling Coaches Association's Lawsuit Is Dismissed." *Education Law Reporter,* 2004, *182*(1), 683–704.

Favia v. Indiana University of Pennsylvania, 812 F. Supp. 578 (W.D. Pa. 1993a).

Favia v. Indiana University of Pennsylvania, 7 F.3d 332 (3rd Cir. 1993b).

Franklin v. Gwinnett County Public Schools, 503 U.S. 60 (1992).

Harper v. Board of Regents of Illinois State University, 35 F. Supp. 2d 1118, 1120 (C.D. Ill. 1999).

Harris, M. "Hitting 'Em Where It Hurts: Using Title IX Litigation to Bring Gender Equity to Athletics." *Denver University Law Review,* 1994, *72*(1), 57–112.

Johnson, J. "Title IX and Intercollegiate Athletics: Current Judicial Interpretations of the Standards for Compliance." *Boston University Law Review,* 1994, *74,* 553–589.

Kelley v. Board of Trustees University of Illinois, 35 F.3d 265 (7th Cir. 1994).

Lamber, J. "Gender and Intercollegiate Athletics: Data and Myths." *University of Michigan Journal of Law Reform,* 2000, *34*(1), 151–230.

Miami University Wrestling Club v. Miami University, 302 F.3d 608 (6th Cir. 2002).

National Collegiate Athletic Association. "NCAA Leadership Groups Urge Department of Education to Rescind Additional Clarification for Title IX and Maintain 1996 Clarification." Indianapolis, Ind.: National Collegiate Athletic Association, 2005.

National Women's Law Center. *Barriers to Fair Play.* Washington, D.C.: National Women's Law Center, 2007. Retrieved Apr. 23, 2008, from http://www.nwlc.org/pdf/BarriersToFairPlay.pdf.

Neal v. Board of Trustees of California State University, No. CV-F-97–5009, 1997 WL 1524813 (E.D. Cal. Dec. 26, 1997).

Neal v. Board of Trustees of the California State Universities, 198 F.3d 763 (9th Cir. 1999).

Office for Civil Rights. "Clarification of Intercollegiate Athletics Policy Guidance: The Three-Part Test." Washington, D.C.: U.S. Department of Education, 1996. Retrieved Apr. 23, 2008, from http://www.ed.gov/print/about/offices/list/ocr/docs/clarific.html.

Office for Civil Rights. "Additional Clarification of Intercollegiate Athletics Policy: Three-Part Test—Part Three." Washington, D.C.: U.S. Department of Education, 2005. Retrieved Apr. 23, 2008, from http://www.ed.gov/about/offices/list/ocr/docs/title9guidanceadditional.html.

Pederson v. Louisiana State University, 912 F. Supp. 892 (M.D. La. 1996).
Pederson v. Louisiana State University, 213 F.3d 858 (5th Cir. 2000).
Roberts v. Colorado State University, 814 F. Supp. 1507 (D. Colo. 1993a).
Roberts v. Colorado State Board of Agriculture, 998 F.2d 824 (10th Cir. 1993b).
Sabo, D., and Grant, C. "Limitations of the Department of Education's Online Survey Method for Measuring Athletic Interest and Ability on U.S.A. Campuses." Retrieved Apr. 23, 2008, from http://www.dyc.edu/crpash/limits_of_online_survey.pdf.
Stevens, L. "The Sports of Numbers: Manipulating Title IX to Rationalize Discrimination Against Women." *Brigham Young University Education and Law Journal,* 2004, *1,* 155–189.
Suggs, W. *A Place on the Team: The Triumph and Tragedy of Title IX.* Princeton, N.J.: Princeton University Press, 2005.
Title IX of the Education Amendments, 20 U.S.C. sec. 1681 (1972).
Title IX, 20 U.S.C. sec. 168(a) (1988).
Title IX Regulation, 44 Fed. Reg. 71413–71423 (1979).
U.S. Department of Education. *Title IX: 25 Years of Progress.* Washington, DC: U.S. Department of Education, 1997. Retrieved Apr. 23, 2008, from http:www.ed.gov/pubs/TitleIX/index.html.

JOHN J. CHESLOCK is an assistant professor in the Center for the Study of Higher Education at the University of Arizona.

SUZANNE E. ECKES is an assistant professor in the Educational Leadership and Policy Studies Department at Indiana University.

NEW DIRECTIONS FOR INSTITUTIONAL RESEARCH • DOI: 10.1002/ir

This chapter addresses the role of personnel data systems in addressing allegations of employment discrimination.

Organization and Maintenance of Data in Employment Discrimination Litigation

Bruce A. Christenson, Kathleen M. Maher, Lorin M. Mueller

Modern organizations such as institutions of higher education characteristically include various administrative offices that gather and maintain records on employees and applicants for employment as part of their normal course of business. Most moderate and large-scale institutions, for example, have a human resource (HR) office that maintains electronic or paper records related to hiring, performance, promotion, and other personnel actions and a payroll department that maintains pay and benefits records. The objective of such record keeping is generally that of promoting efficient and effective management of an institution and meeting legally mandated reporting requirements. Although not originally collected for the purpose of addressing allegations of discrimination, these data can be an excellent source of information for such investigations to the extent that they record the details of various personnel actions and employee compensation.

This chapter discusses the organization and maintenance of personnel data in addressing allegations of employment discrimination. Specifically, we describe the designs of an employee history database, an applicant flow database, and a qualifications database and outline how institutional

research offices can use these databases to conduct inquiries into possible problems at the institution that could lead to litigation.

Overview

Administrative data on employees and applicants for employment can be used to provide anecdotal evidence or bring rigorous statistical analysis to bear on disputes over allegedly discriminatory personnel practices. Such disputes can be raised under various equal employment opportunity (EEO) laws with differing provisions, of which Title VII is the most comprehensive (Gutman, 2000).

Two broad theories of discrimination under Title VII that courts have recognized are disparate treatment and disparate impact. In brief, disparate treatment refers to intentional actions by a decision maker that favor members of one group over another. Disparate impact, more commonly called adverse impact, occurs when an employer institutes a practice that results in the selection (hiring, promotion, and so on) of one group at a substantially lower rate than a favored group. In adverse impact cases, there is no need to demonstrate intent on behalf of the employer, and the disputed employment practices are thought to be facially neutral (i.e., they do not appear to discriminate on their face, as opposed to being obviously discriminatory).

Evaluating these types of claims requires employers to maintain different types of data. For disparate treatment, unless there is direct evidence of discrimination (for example, a decision maker admitting to discrimination), claims must be evaluated on the basis of comparing the qualifications of those alleging discrimination to the qualifications of those selected (or to the job requirements if no one is selected). Evaluating such claims requires fairly detailed information regarding applicant qualifications and the requirements of the job at the time of the selection.

Adverse impact does not require extensive information on the qualifications of each applicant. In fact, some researchers contend that relative qualifications should have no bearing on the evaluation of adverse impact claims (Siskin and Trippi, 2005), although this seems to be too broad of a generalization for these authors. However, evaluating adverse impact claims requires more finely detailed information regarding the point at which applicants were eliminated from consideration. In other words, evaluating adverse impact claims requires the investigator to know the specific personnel practice that is responsible for screening out each applicant. (See *Connecticut v. Teal*, 1982, for a discussion of this requirement from a case law perspective.)

In the abstract, it may seem trivial to collect and maintain the data required to evaluate both of these types of claims. In practice, however, it may be very difficult to maintain records that provide both the rich qualifications information required to evaluate disparate treatment claims and the

NEW DIRECTIONS FOR INSTITUTIONAL RESEARCH • DOI: 10.1002/ir

precise information regarding personnel decisions required to examine adverse impact claims.

Illustrative Databases

This section describes three types of databases commonly used in employment litigation settings. The first is the employee history database, which details the employees within an organization and describes their roles in the organization (such as position, level or grade, unit, and supervisor). The second is an applicant flow database, which details the applicants to each opening in an organization, who was hired, and any decisions that led to the final candidate pools. The third is a qualifications database that details the education, training, relevant work experience, and other factors for each applicant to a position. Although beyond the scope of this chapter, other databases can also prove valuable to institutions for litigation. Payroll records, for example, are often among the best maintained records on employees. A payroll database can supplement information in the databases described in this chapter or be useful in settlement negotiations.

Employee History Database. An employee history database (EHDB) records the work experiences of individual employees in an organization's workforce over a designated period of time. The database includes information on selected characteristics of individual employees and the personnel actions they have experienced during their tenure with the organization. Bessey (1991) provides a comprehensive discussion of how to build and check an employee history file for analysis in an employment discrimination lawsuit. She maintains that an EHDB is one of the "most essential elements" in employment discrimination cases because it keeps track of the day-to-day status of employees over long periods of time. She notes that analysts can use this type of file to analyze a variety of issues that appear in employment discrimination cases, such as:

- Representation of protected class members in the work force,
- Extent to which class members receive their fair share of promotions or supervisory training,
- Whether class members wait longer to receive their promotions,
- Whether class members receive lower wages than nonclass members, and
- Whether differing qualifications between class members and nonclass members can account for any observed disparities [1991, p. 283].

The employee characteristics that are included in an EHDB tend to be static, whereas information pertaining to personnel actions is dynamic in nature. This distinction supports organizing the EHDB into two related files or relational data tables. Employee characteristics that are not likely to change (such as gender, race, and birth date) can be maintained in an

Table 4.1. Sample Employee Directory

Record Number	Name	ID Number	Gender	Race	Birth Date
1	Aguilar Diane A	12378	F	Hispanic	September 15, 1980
2	Cho Jin Ying	33479	F	Asian	August 01, 1975
3	Colemann Garry	14889	M	Black	December 01, 1967
4	Hernandez Rosa	11399	F	Hispanic	August 01, 1960
5	Klooney Rose M	24842	F	White	June 01, 1962
6	Pfiler Terry A	28775	M	White	February 01, 1977

employee directory with one record per individual, as represented in Table 4.1. The name and randomly assigned identifications could be kept in a separate file to protect confidentiality, with only the identification number appearing in the directory.

The second file, referred to as the employee history, is a transaction-based file. In this file, each personnel action is represented by a separate transaction record. When two different personnel actions occur on the same date, two transaction records are created—one for each personnel action. Table 4.2 is a simplified example of the history records for a single individual—in this case, a faculty member. The employee history file is linked to the employee directory by a unique identification number that appears in both tables. The transaction records are entered in the order in which the actions occurred on that date.

The researcher must select the employee characteristics, personnel actions, and information associated with personnel actions to include in the database. That information needs to be tailored to the actual or potential allegations of discrimination and the organizational context. Bessey (1991) groups common variables pertaining to employee characteristics and personnel actions based on their typical importance into three categories: absolutely needed, usually needed, and those that may be needed based on allegations and planned analysis. The variables that are absolutely needed are employee name, employee identification number, class membership (as related to an allegation or research question), typically major personnel actions (hires, promotions, demotions, and discharges or departures), effective dates of action, and the positions and occupations held after the action. Some of the variables that are usually needed include alternate names and spellings, date of birth, a variety of other personnel actions (for example, changes in specific job title, change in salary, temporary promotions or demotions) and associated dates, and salary level. Other useful variables might be educational attainment, level of job held prior to hiring, amount of relevant experience before being hired, typically minor personnel actions (including monetary and nonmonetary awards, leave without pay, change in location within an organization, and training) and

NEW DIRECTIONS FOR INSTITUTIONAL RESEARCH • DOI: 10.1002/ir

Table 4.2. Sample Employee History

Record Number	ID Number	Effective Date	Type of Action	Department	Job Title	Appointment Type	Teaching Units	Other Units	Salary
1	24842	August 01, 1997	Hire—tenure track	Psychology	Assistant professor	Tenure track	15.0	0.0	$48,000
2	24842	December 01, 1997	Faculty research award	Psychology	Assistant professor	Tenure track	12.0	3.0	48,000
3	24842	August 01, 1999	Extension—tenure track	Psychology	Assistant professor	Tenure track	15.0	0.0	51,916
4	24842	January 01, 2000	Research grant award	Psychology	Assistant professor	Tenure track	9.0	6.0	51,916
5	24842	August 01, 2001	Extension—tenure track	Psychology	Assistant professor	Tenure track	9.0	6.0	58,333
6	24842	August 01, 2002	Tenure awarded	Psychology	Assistant professor	Tenured	15.0	0.0	64,168
7	24842	August 01, 2002	Promotion	Psychology	Associate professor	Tenured	15.0	0.0	64,168
8	24842	August 01, 2004	Sabbatical award	Psychology	Associate professor	Tenured	0.0	15.0	81,010
9	24842	January 01, 2005	Return	Psychology	Associate professor	Tenured	15.0	0.0	81,010
10	24842	January 01, 2005	Research grant award	Psychology	Associate professor	Tenured	9.0	6.0	81,010
11	24842	August 01, 2005	Promotion	Psychology	Full professor	Tenured	9.0	6.0	89,111

NEW DIRECTIONS FOR INSTITUTIONAL RESEARCH • DOI: 10.1002/ir

associated dates, organizational units or locations, amounts of awards, and types of training. Whether a particular personnel action is considered major or minor depends on the allegations, issues, and planned analyses.

In determining the scope of the EHDB, the researcher needs to ensure it covers the relevant workforce and time period. The relevant workforce may or may not include all the employees in an organization. In employment discrimination class actions, a class may include only a portion of the institution's workforce, defined, for example, by occupation, specific job levels or positions in the organization, departments, or other organizational units. All employees who are potential class members, as well as employees in similar situations who are not potential class members, need to be included in the database. The definition of the relevant workforce depends on the specific allegations or issues being examined. For example, if promotions within a unit are open to employees within the organization but in a different unit, the database should contain eligible individuals from other organizational units.

The time period covered by an EHDB depends on a combination of factors, including the timing of the alleged discriminatory practices that are at issue and whether information prior to the occurrence of those events is needed to establish the proper groupings or pools of employees within which to analyze the allegedly discriminatory practices. The time frame for the alleged discriminatory practices may be a point of contention that needs to be resolved by the court. In cases where the allegedly discriminatory employment practice is ongoing, the time period covered by the EHDB may include the period during which the case works its way through the administrative hearing process of the Equal Employment Opportunity Commission (EEOC) and onto the court calendar.

Although organizations are increasingly computerizing their record keeping, source documents that might be used to create an EHDB are often maintained in paper format or as electronic images of paper documents. Thus, it is important to consider the advantages and limitations of relying on existing computer files and returning to source documents when compiling information for an EHDB (Bessey, 1991).

Applicant Flow Database. The purpose of an applicant flow database (AFDB) is to gather together the information that is processed during consideration for a job opening, promotional opportunity, or other competitive selection decision. When promotions are considered individually, based on an individual's performance rather than on a specific opening, one would not typically consider these opportunities as part of the applicant flow process. This process generally consists of a number of steps that begin with applications being submitted and end with the selection of one or more applicants for the position. However, there may be cases that end without selection when no candidate was well qualified or the announcement was cancelled. In general, the institution will post an announcement for a position opening, applicants will apply, candidates will be evaluated, and a candidate will be hired.

NEW DIRECTIONS FOR INSTITUTIONAL RESEARCH • DOI: 10.1002/ir

Although this is admittedly an oversimplification, the steps and information related to the processing of the steps in an applicant flow process can be usefully separated into three main components: (1) information pertaining to each vacancy announcement; (2) information about the participants in the process, including applicants, hiring managers, and other hiring officials; and (3) information about the rating and selection process. Each institution may have additional steps or perform some steps in a slightly different order. In some cases, the process employed by the organization may change over time or in reaction to the specific conditions of an opening. The database structure should, if possible, capture these changes.

When an open position is identified, the first step of the process is the announcement of the opening. The announcement generally contains the following information: announcement number and title; job title; job description; minimum qualifications (knowledge, skills, and abilities); educational requirements; additional desired knowledge, skills, and abilities; number of openings; and closing date for the acceptance of applications. Other information may include the location of the opening (department, for example), whether relocation assistance is available, or any special circumstances of the position, such as a temporary assignment or part-time position. This then defines the first component of the AFDB, which we will refer to as the openings file.

An openings file generally contains one record per job announcement and all the information in the job announcement. It also contains other important information, such as hiring manager, interviewers, and information related to decisions about the announcement that does not vary by applicant or selection. For example, sometimes there are no qualified candidates for the opening, or because of fiscal decisions, the announcement is cancelled. It is important to track this information even when no hiring or promotion decision is made.

In some cases, the openings file may be better maintained in a number of small relational tables. One important piece of information associated with each announcement is the job description. This may be several paragraphs of text that could be useful for content analyses or other kinds of anecdotal review. However, it is likely that for the hiring and promotion process, HR staff have already extracted key knowledge, skills, or abilities (KSAs) that are required or desired for the position. Thus, the openings file could include that extracted information and the job description could be maintained in a separate table.

Table 4.3 displays a subset of information that might be contained in an openings file. The column headings are a sample of the type of announcement information. The table body identifies the participants involved in evaluating applications and making decisions throughout the selection process.

After the announcement of a position opening, applicants may apply to the position. The announcement typically includes specific requirements

Table 4.3. Sample Data in an Openings File

Announcement Number	Job Title	Opening Date	Closing Date	Salary (Range)	Number of Vacancies	Status	Cancellation Reason
				Announcement Information			
2006-1666	Administrative Assistant II	09/25/2006	10/09/2006	Commensurate with knowledge and experience	1	Cancelled	Funding withdrawn
2006-1667	Administrative Analyst/Specialist	10/06/2006	10/20/2006	$3,137–$5,019/month	2	Filled	

Announcement Number	HR Specialist	HR Extension	Hiring Manager (ID Number)	Interviewer 1 (ID Number)	Interviewer 2 (ID Number)	Interviewer 3 (ID Number)
			Evaluator Information			
2006-1666	Virginia Garnica	1567	Robert Montgomery (2987)	Robert Montgomery (2987)	Ramon Aguilar (2977)	Candi Hagerty (2980)
2006-1667	Virginia Garnica	1567	Kellie Maher (3543)	Robert Koehler (3501)	Marc Segal (3588)	Luci Rositano (3553)

New Directions for Institutional Research • DOI: 10.1002/ir

regarding the information each applicant is expected to provide and a date by which this information needs to be submitted. Thus, the second component of the AFDB is the applicants file. Each application should be assigned an identification number, so that over time, different applications from the same individual can be identified separately. In addition, using an application number rather than name makes it easier to keep individual information confidential, as well as distinguishing candidates with similar names to avoid confusion. The applicants file then includes the following kinds of information: announcement number, applicant number, name, address, contact information, and other demographic data. Table 4.4 presents some of the variables included in an applicant file in a series of three panels, including the identification number assigned to each application and identifying information about the applicant such as name, social security number, home address, and race.

The applicants file includes one record for each candidate for each job announcement and information about the candidate that relates to the opening. This could include type and dates of academic degrees earned, KSAs that are either listed on the application or are extracted from a résumé, and special licenses or certificates such as state bar, CPA, and Certified Network Engineer (see panel B of Table 4.4).

Frequently an efficient way to organize the AFDB is to include information regarding how each application was handled within the applicants file. A variable for separable decisions in the hiring process is recorded in the general order in which they occur. For example, after each applicant submits an application, an HR professional screens the résumé to determine whether a candidate is qualified and then decides whether to pass the application on to a hiring manager, who then invites promising candidates in for an interview. The hiring manager selects from the interviewed candidates. In this case, we would expect to see at least three variables corresponding to (1) whether the HR professional found the applicant to be qualified, (2) whether the candidate was interviewed, and (3) whether the candidate was selected. Recording this information for each specific step is critical for identifying steps in the hiring process that may be susceptible to legal challenge. It is becoming increasingly important to record declinations and withdrawals at each stage of the process (such as declining an interview), as the effort required to apply to multiple job openings decreases through the use of electronic résumés and online recruitment databases.

In larger selection systems, it may be that some highly repetitive information on individual applicants can be better maintained in a set of smaller related tables. For example, if applicants are applying to multiple openings while retaining the same home address, it might be more efficient to keep a directory of the names and addresses of applicants in a separate table along with a unique identification number for each individual. The unique identification number would link to a table showing the disposition of each of the applications for that individual (see panel C in Table 4.4). This would

Table 4.4. Sample Data in an Applicants File

Panel A: Application IDs and Applicant Identifiers

Announcement Number	Application Number	Name	Individual's ID Number	Street	City	State	Zip	Date Received	Race
2006-1666	06-23871	Williams, Paul	3485	134 Hallmark Dr.	San Francisco	CA	94123	10/05/2006	Black
2006-1666	06-23957	Dalldorf, Jonathan	4567	847 23rd Ave.	San Jose	CA	94011	10/08/2006	White
2006-1666	06-24111	Chang, PiLing	3233	1919 Main St.	Redwood City	CA	94062	10/08/2006	Asian
2006-1666	06-24345	Bush, Barbara	4565	2424 King Ave.	Belmont	CA	94002	10/09/2006	Black
2006-1666	06-24368	Smith, Alexander	9786	4949 Centennial Dr.	Santa Clara	CA	94334	10/12/2006	White
2006-1667	06-23788	Miller, Janet	6587	2044 Palm Ave.	Redwood City	CA	94061	10/05/2006	White
2006-1667	06-23901	Darko, Kyna	2906	2387 19th Ave. #6	San Francisco	CA	94122	10/05/2006	White
2006-1667	06-24074	Osborne, Robert	5249	708 Woodside Rd.	Hillsdale	CA	94444	10/08/2006	Black
2006-1667	06-24398	Gendotti, Lisa Marie	8213	2610 Carson St.	Palo Alto	CA	94305	10/10/2006	Other
2006-1667	06-24687	Avalar, Jennifer	6872	1594 Hudson St.	San Francisco	CA	94125	10/11/2006	Hispanic
2006-1667	06-24701	White, Julia	5301	1880 Holly Ave.	San Carlos	CA	94070	10/11/2006	Black

Panel B: Educational Background of Applicants

Application Number	Degree 1	Degree 1 Date	Degree 2	Degree 2 Date	Degree 3	Degree 3 Date
06-23871	A.A.	12/1987	B.A.	06/1990		
06-23957	B.A.	06/2002	M.A.	12/2004		
06-24111	A.A.	08/1981	B.A.	12/1983	J.D.	06/1987
06-24345	Cert.	06/2006				

NEW DIRECTIONS FOR INSTITUTIONAL RESEARCH • DOI: 10.1002/ir

06-24368	B.A.		06/2005	M.A.	06/2007			
06-23788								
06-23901	A.A.		06/1999	Cert.	12/1999	Cert.	06/2000	No
06-24064	B.A.		12/1993					
06-24398	AA.		06/2003	B.A.	05/2005			
06-24687	B.A.		06/1985	M.B.A.	06/2001			
06-24701	A.A.		06/1985	B.A.	12/1988	J.D.	05/2004	

Panel C: Disposition of Applications

Announcement Number	Application Number	Qualified	Reason Not Qualified	Qualified (Q) or Highly Qualified (HQ)	Interviewed	Current Employee?	Selected?	Placed?
2006-1666	06-23871	Yes		Q	Yes		Yes	No
2006-1666	06-23957	Yes		Q	Yes		No	
2006-1666	06-24111	Yes		Q	Declined			
2006-1666	06-24345	No	Lacks education					
2006-1666	06-24368	No	Late application					
2006-1667	06-23788	Yes		HQ	Yes	Yes	Declined	
2006-1667	06-23901	Yes		HQ	Yes	Yes	Yes	Yes
2006-1667	06-24074	Yes		Q	No	No	No	
2006-1667	06-24398	No	Lacks experience			No		
2006-1667	06-24687	Yes		HQ	Yes	No	Yes	Yes
2006-1667	06-24701	Yes		Q	Yes	No	No	

New Directions for Institutional Research • DOI: 10.1002/ir

also help researchers maintain the confidentiality of the personal information of applicants.

In more complex situations, the same or similar announcements may be used to gather applicant pools for multiple openings within an organization. For example, consider the process of hiring administrative support staff for a new department. Applications might be gathered for multiple hiring managers based on the same announcement. Although these pools are often similar, they are not always identical. Specifically, candidates who are selected are not entered back into the applicant pool for positions filled later. Other candidates may be excluded for consideration after declining an offer, making a bad impression, or taking another position in the organization.

In these cases, it may be efficient to create a referral file that records differences in the hiring managers, selection criteria, and position-specific information. Each row in the referral file corresponds to a set of rows in the applicants file (in other words, all applicants considered in that particular referral) and a single row in the openings file.

Qualifications Database.   Related to the AFDB is the qualifications database (QDB), a compilation of the attributes of either employees already in positions or applicants to positions. Beyond attributes delineated by the announcement, the QDB is used to compile a broader range of attributes or construct composites of qualifications. Qualifications data are particularly useful in pattern and practice claims of hiring and compensation discrimination, where a potentially discriminatory decision may be explained through analyses of relevant qualifications of candidates. Chapters Five and Six in this volume provide introductions to these analyses. To better understand the construction of the QDB, consider the question, "Do the KSAs used to hire or promote employees adequately identify the KSAs of the position?" To answer this question, one could look to employees who have held positions during a specific period.

One resource is the EHDB, which contains the job history for all employees during their tenure in the organization. For every position of interest, the EHDB provides information about positions held, awards received, and education. Thus, the QDB can be built first from the EHDB. Rather than looking at specific skills delineated in a résumé or application, the EHDB shows previous jobs within the organization. The researcher can construct attributes such as lower-level jobs in the same position, same-level jobs in related positions, jobs held in a lower or the same level in a broader category of related positions (job family), and education variables.

Qualifications databases take many forms. In some cases, they may be very small, precise databases designed to investigate differences in qualifications within a limited set of positions or jobs. In this case, we would expect to find fields that correspond to specific skills, training, and work experience or performance. Here we might observe specific training courses, job rotation schedules, performance awards, and even skills as fields in the database. We could anticipate that the records in these cases will need to be very precise,

New Directions for Institutional Research • DOI: 10.1002/ir

such as recording months or weeks of job experience. This kind of database might be used to examine pay equity among employees within a job family, for example.

In other cases, the QDB may be used to examine the role of qualifications across a wide variety of jobs and job families and therefore is not expected to be as detailed in terms of specific job skills. In this case, the database could include the major field of study in which a degree has been earned, years of experience in a particular job or related types of jobs (referred to as a job family in the federal civil service), years of experience with the organization, and some gross measures of professional development (such as the number of training courses taken). If particular sets of skills are critical to a large number of jobs within the scope of the investigation, they could be included as fields in the database. For example, it would be prudent to include a training course (such as how to use a new software program) that could relate to large differences in performance ratings and outcomes of valued personnel actions. In some cases, work experiences may simply be recorded as whether an individual has a particular amount of experience within a related set of jobs (for example, one year). An example of when this type of database might be consulted is when basic employment screens are used across a broad class of jobs (such as screening résumés for basic educational and work experience requirements for all jobs within an organization).

Relative to the AFDB, which may show that two candidates have bachelor's degrees, the QDB would also indicate their fields of study and how long ago they earned the degree. Similarly, the QDB would indicate how long an employee held a lower-level position, a similar position at the same level, or a position in the same job family.

It is worth noting here that it is not the role of the database creator to determine the predictive validity or job relevance of the data recorded in the fields of the QDB. This decision is a scientific and legal question; a qualified HR administrator may be able to determine the appropriateness of each piece of information for making personnel decisions at a later time. The role of the database creator is to record all relevant qualifications that are believed to have been factored in when making personnel decisions.

Addressing Missing and Incomplete Data on Race/Ethnicity and Gender

The correct assignment of race/ethnicity and gender to individuals is particularly important because these are two of the protected categories frequently referenced in complaints of discrimination based on Title VII. Even a small percentage of inconsistent or missing data on employees or applicants can have an important impact on the analysis.

Federal record-keeping and reporting requirements frame institutional efforts to maintain information on the race/ethnicity and gender of employees. Employers with one hundred or more employees, for example, are required under Title VII to file an annual report, referred to as an EEO-1 Report, showing the relationship of minority and female workers to the employer's total workforce in specified job categories.[1] Although exempt from filing EEO-1 reports, institutions of higher education are required to file biennial staffing reports that show, among other things, the representation of minorities and females among faculty and staff. The reports are filed with the National Center for Education Statistics.[2]

Race/Ethnicity. Self-identification is the preferred method for classifying the race/ethnicity of individual employees. For several decades, federal employees have been asked to provide voluntary self-identification through Standard Form 181 of the Office of Personnel Management. Staff members at educational institutions typically self-identify when they are employed or submit an application for employment. The concept of self-identification was reinforced by the Office of Management and Budget (OMB) in its 1997 revision of standards for collecting and reporting data on race and ethnicity.[3] When an employee or applicant chooses not to self-identify, visual observation by a third party may be used to identify an employee or applicant. It can be harder to provide third-party identification for applicants, as they may never be seen by HR or other university or college officials.

At times personnel records may contain inconsistent data on the race/ethnicity identity of an employee or the information may be missing. In cases of inconsistent information, records that are known to be based on self-identification would take precedent over those based on observation or of unknown origin. Thus, in addition to classifying employees, it is also useful to maintain information on the basis of that classification.

In cases where inconsistent records are all based on self-identification, the current or most recently reported race may be the most appropriate. However, such inconsistencies might also indicate that a person identifies with more than one race. Although it has been recognized for some time that individuals may identify with more than one race, incorporating this awareness into the collection and classification of data on race/ethnicity is still evolving.

The revised standards for the collection and reporting of race and ethnicity data that OMB issued in 1997 required that individuals have the opportunity to identify themselves with more than one race. OMB increased the minimum number of racial categories from four to five by separating the Asian and Pacific Islander category into two separate categories: one for "Asian" and another for "Native Hawaiian and Other Pacific Islander" (the other three categories are American Indian or Alaska Native, Black or African American, and White). Organizations are strongly encouraged to use a two-question format for collecting race/ethnicity data that would begin by asking individuals to indicate whether they are Hispanic or Latino and then ask individuals to select one or more race categories.

NEW DIRECTIONS FOR INSTITUTIONAL RESEARCH • DOI: 10.1002/ir

The U.S. Department of Education is requiring educational institutions to allow staff to identify with more than one race and meet the other minimum standards set by OMB. The underlying databases and methods of collection are expected to accommodate all possible combinations, although not all need to be reported. The reporting on race and ethnicity is expected to change in 2009. Beyond the race/ethnicity classifications commonly recognized by the EEOC, the Integrated Post Secondary Education Data System Survey's Fall Staffing Survey also includes race/ethnicity categories for "nonresident alien" and "race-ethnicity unknown."

When race/ethnicity information on an employee is inconsistent or missing, it is preferable to resurvey the employee if consulting with him or her does not conflict with an active legal case. Following the adoption of the new standards for collecting and recording race/ethnicity data, the National Center for Education Statistics is encouraging educational institutions to allow all current staff to reidentify their race/ethnicity using the new standards. However, it may be necessary in active litigation involving potential class members to ask an HR official, supervisor, or manager who is familiar with an employee to provide identification. It is important to confirm that this official is familiar with the employee and is not simply reporting what he or she recalls from an official record, unless that record can be shown to be a self-identification.

When data are missing or inconsistent for employees who are no longer with an organization, an HR official, manager, or supervisor who worked with the former employee might be asked to provide identification. Except perhaps in cases of active litigation, a coworker might also be asked to provide identification. Identification might be found in past employment or other official records. For instance, an employee may have self-identified his or her race/ethnicity by statements made in a previously filed grievance. Racial identification has even been obtained from death certificates of former employees who are deceased.

Gender. As with race/ethnicity, self-identification of an employee or applicant's gender is preferred, although visual identification is also acceptable. When the information for a current employee is missing or inconsistent, the employee might be asked to self-identify as part of updating personnel records so long as this does not conflict with ongoing litigation. For former employees, gender might be inferred from documents in the personnel file that were prepared by the employee. For example, an individual may use the title of "Mr." or "Ms." on an application or letter. However, caution should be used in relying on documents prepared by employers to resolve uncertainty over the gender of an employee, as the employer may have incorrectly inferred the information from the employee's name. Bessey (1991) maintains that names of employees should never be used to make official attribution of gender in gender-based discrimination cases, as errors are likely if androgynous or unfamiliar names are encountered. Instead it is better to confirm with an

HR official, manager, or supervisor who worked with the individual, so as to minimize the possibility of misattributing gender.

Using Data to Monitor Equity: Self-Critical Analysis

This section describes the role of the databases in complying with equal employment opportunity law, performing with respect to affirmative action plans, and generally maintaining equity within the workforce. The method described here, self-critical analysis, entails identifying areas of organizational risk and gathering information to examine the personnel processes that may have an impact on maintaining an equitable work environment.

A self-critical analysis may be conducted to review the employment practices of an organization and the effects of those practices on the diversity of its workforce. Often, in order to conduct such an analysis, more data are required than the organization collects to meet government reporting requirements. The databases described in this chapter can be used to determine whether statistically significant disparities exist in employing minorities and women in relation to their availability in the local labor market.

Most large organizations are required to file EEO reports reflecting the gender, racial, and ethnic makeup of their workforce. If for any of the jobs or job groups included in the report there are large shortfalls for any particular protected group, then the organization is expected to take steps, including the establishment of goals and the implementation of recruitment, selection, and retention strategies, for eliminating the shortfalls. Unfortunately, if there are shortfalls, the standard analytical approach used to develop standard EEO reports (an eight-factor availability analysis followed by a utilization analysis), which looks only at who is in the workforce, not at the applicants for positions, does not give any information regarding the reason for the shortfall. In addition, EEO reports, because of the relatively broad job groupings they use, can disguise critical problems in hiring and promoting individuals from protected groups.

When monitoring how well the organization is currently doing, as opposed to how well it has done over time, the best data come from an applicant flow analysis. Therefore, it may be preferable for an organization to maintain an AFDB in order to facilitate monitoring hiring practices. Only a properly conducted applicant flow analysis, based on a complete AFDB, can provide information on why the shortfalls exist and inform decisions about what steps should be taken to overcome the shortfalls. If it is not possible to carry out an applicant flow analysis, an availability analysis might focus on recent selections rather than relying on the standard analyses included in the annual EEO reports.

In addition to recording who applied for each position at an organization, a complete AFDB also contains information on how far each applicant proceeded through the selection process. This is important, because the typical employee selection process contains multiple steps, some under the control of the organization and some under the control of the applicant. For example, the decision not to take a required medical test is a decision that is under the control of the applicant; the decision that an applicant who took the medical test did not pass is a decision that is under the control of the organization. By maintaining all the information in an AFDB, it is possible to carry out an analysis to tease out the reasons for any disparities.

Just as an AFDB allows the appropriate analysis of the outcomes for individuals who applied for positions with an organization, a transactional EHDB permits the development and presentation of detailed pictures of the course of the work history of individual employees or groups of employees. These data permit the analysis of such matters as promotion rates for cohorts of employees who entered the same position at approximately the same time, as well as differences in the mean time between promotions for employees in the same position. Perhaps most important, an employee history database can be of great importance if there are issues related to different employees, or different groups of employees, having different levels of qualifications and thus being treated differently.

An organization might wish to conduct a self-critical analysis for any job or job family that is part of the organization's affirmative action plan, has a high number of selections, or has general concerns that there is the possibility of differential selection rates. The self-critical analysis would take the form of a report examining the selections for the jobs in question and identifying areas of risk for the organization. The analysis might begin with an analysis of each individual hiring decision and look across multiple groups (for example, gender and major ethnic groups) to determine if any selection events appear by themselves to warrant further review. After reviewing individual selection events, the organization may wish to aggregate results by job family, organizational unit or department, or other grouping of interest to determine if there is a larger pattern of adverse employment actions within any meaningful grouping. The organization might use a number of potential criteria to determine which employment actions to examine, but certainly any employment action (or aggregate) that reaches the level of significance should be reviewed, as should any that result in a selection rate for any group of less than four-fifths of a favored group. Organizations may want to use substantially more liberal criteria, in consultation with an experienced analyst. The criteria cited here are the strictest ones. The organization should conduct these analyses for each separable step in the selection process, and possibly for noncompetitive processes including promotions and tenure reviews.

It may be preferable to conduct these reviews on a frequent basis, such as once a year. First and foremost, the events and factors that led to any particular employment action are likely to be relatively fresh in people's minds. Second, in the event an employment action is determined to be improper, the organization can act in a timely manner to minimize damages. Finally, the organization is able to detect potential issues before it incurs any legal liability and act to correct them.

Self-critical analyses can be risky for organizations because the information they generate may be considered discoverable in legal proceedings. Lindemann and Grossman (2007) observe that courts have yet to take a definitive position regarding the existence of a privilege for information containing self-critical analyses. They note that some courts have treated self-critical analyses as privileged, while holding that the objective data underlying the self-critical analyses are discoverable (for example, *Penk* v. *Oregon State Board of Higher Education*, 1982). They also report that other courts have refused to recognize any form of self-critical privilege, such as the U.S. District Court for the Northern District of California, which maintained that a self-critical analysis privilege does not exist in Title VII cases (such as *Granberry* v. *Jet Blue Airways*, 2005). Of particular significance for institutions of higher education, Lindemann and Grossman report that the courts do not generally recognize academic privilege for peer review documentation. They cite *University of Pennsylvania* v. *EEOC* (1990) in which the Supreme Court affirmed that "plaintiffs showing of relevance is sufficient to require disclosure of peer-review materials pertinent to charges of discrimination challenging tenure decisions" (Lindeman and Grossman, 2007, p. 2248).

Although there is some risk to generating analyses that may be used in a legal setting as evidence against the organization, we believe that these concerns overlook the substantial risk posed by failing to critically evaluate the potential for discrimination in employment decisions. Specifically, organizations have a legal obligation to institute fair and nondiscriminatory hiring practices, and this obligation does not go away if the organization chooses not to examine the data.

Conclusion

Although not originally collected for the purpose of addressing actual or potential allegations of discrimination, personnel and other administrative records are an excellent source of data for investigating such concerns, as they often provide the detailed information regarding personnel actions necessary to make an assessment. The challenge for the researcher is to organize those records in a manner that can address specific legal issues regarding possible differences in the experiences of employees or applicants based on race, sex, or other classes protected under Title VII or other EEO laws. Depending on the law, the underlying issues may concern intentional actions, as reflected in disparate treatment claims or unintended consequences of personnel practices as reflected in disparate or adverse impact claims. While the databases required for employment discrimination cases need to be tailored to the specific claims in a case, three types of databases are commonly useful: an employee history database, an applicant flow database, and a qualifications database.

The accurate identification of race/ethnicity and gender is particularly important because these are two of the protected categories that are frequently the basis of discrimination complaints. Self-identification is the preferred form of identification in both cases. In resolving inconsistencies or minimizing missing data, it may be necessary to rely on third-party identification from HR officials, managers, supervisors, or coworkers who know the individual. Although less reliable, such third-party identification has also been considered acceptable when, for practical or legal reasons, self-identification is not possible. It is important to keep track of the basis of identification, for resolving inconsistencies as self-identification takes precedence over identification by others. In the case of race/ethnicity identification, inconsistent records may also reflect that an employee identifies with more than one group. Recent developments in federal requirements for collecting information on race will allow individuals to identify with more than one race.

Some institutions may wish to conduct self-critical analyses that identify organizational risk with respect to maintaining equity in their personnel practices and workforce. Such analyses will likely focus on jobs or job families as related to an organization's affirmative action plan, or where the organization experiences a high number of selections, or where there is concern over differential selection rates. The databases described in this chapter can be used for conducting these analyses. If analyses are conducted on a regular basis, the events being examined will be more current and therefore more easily recalled. The organization can act in a timely manner to correct any problems and may be able to detect potential issues. While organizations face a risk because the information generated may be considered discoverable in legal proceedings, they are also at risk if they fail to adequately evaluate the potential for discrimination in their employment decisions.

Chapters Five and Six illustrate how these types of databases can be used to analyze employment outcomes for evidence of bias or inequitable treatment of groups of employees.

Notes

1. Equal Employment Opportunity, Standard Form 100, Rev. January 2006, Employer Information Report EEO-1 Instruction Booklet. http://www.eeoc.gov/eeo1/instruction_rev_2006.html

2. The record-keeping and reporting requirements under Title VII and the Americans with Disabilities Act as identified in 29 C.F.R. 1602.50 call for institutions of higher education to submit a biennial Higher Education Staff Information Report EEO-6 to the EEOC or its delegate. In 1993, the National Center for Education Statistics of the Department of Education assumed responsibility for compiling this information and replaced the EEO-6 with a new reporting form, the Integrated Post Secondary Education Data System Survey (IPEDS), which consists of nine components, one of which is the Fall Staff Survey that is completed in odd-numbered years (http://www.nces.ed.gov/ipeds).

NEW DIRECTIONS FOR INSTITUTIONAL RESEARCH • DOI: 10.1002/ir

3. "Revisions to the Standards for the Classification of Federal Data on Race and Ethnicity," *Federal Register,* Oct. 30, 1997, p. 58781. http://www.whitehouse.gov/omb/fedreg/1997standards.html

References

Bessey, B. "Employee History File: Essential Element in Employment Discrimination Cases." *Trial Lawyers Guide,* 1991, *35*(3), 283–311.

Connecticut v. Teal, 457 U.S. 440, 29 FEP 1 (1982).

Equal Employment Opportunity Commission. *Employer Information Report EEO-1 Instruction Booklet.* Jan. 2006. Retrieved October 5, 2007, from http://www.eeoc.gov/eeo1/instruction_rev_2006.html.

Granberry v. Jet Blue Airways, 228 F.R.D. 647 (N.D. Cal. 2005).

Gutman, A. *EEO Law and Personnel Practices.* (2nd ed.) Thousand Oaks, Calif.: Sage, 2000.

Lindemann, B., and Grossman, P. *Employment Discrimination Law.* (4th ed.) Washington, D.C.: BNA Books, 2007.

Office of Management and Budget. "Revisions to the Standards for the Classification of Federal Data on Race and Ethnicity" [Electronic version]. *Federal Register, 62,* 58781, 1997.

Penk v. Oregon State Board of Education, 99 F.R.D. 506, 37 FEP 918 (D. Or. 1982).

Siskin, B., and Trippi, J. "Statistical Issues in Employment Litigation." In F. Landy (ed.), *Employment Discrimination Litigation: Behavioral, Quantitative, and Legal Perspectives.* San Francisco: Jossey-Bass, 2005.

University of Pennsylvania v. EEOC, 493 U.S. 182, 51 FEP 1118 (1990).

BRUCE A. CHRISTENSON *is a principal research scientist with the American Institutes for Research in Washington, D.C.*

KATHLEEN M. MAHER *is a senior research scientist with the American Institutes for Research in Washington, D.C.*

LORIN M. MUELLER *is a senior research scientist with the American Institutes for Research in Washington, D.C.*

Employment decisions like selection, promotion, and termination should be analyzed to prevent litigation or to refute a prima facie case.

Analyzing Personnel Selection Decisions in Employment Discrimination Litigation Settings

Lorin M. Mueller, Eric M. Dunleavy, and Ash K. Buonasera

In many employment discrimination cases, the employment outcome that is the subject of the complaint involves whether employees from a protected group receive the benefit of a particular decision at the same rate as the members of a presumably preferred group. For example, applicants can be hired or not hired, promoted or not promoted, terminated or not terminated, and so on, and the rates of attaining these outcomes (whether positive or negative) may differ across groups. These decisions are evaluated in a substantial portion of all employment discrimination claims (Zink and Gutman, 2005).

This chapter familiarizes readers with how to analyze personnel selection decisions in employment discrimination litigation. Toward that end, we first outline some of the basic legal principles that serve as the basis for analyses related to claims of discriminatory employment practices. Second, we describe how to conduct a scientific investigation of the merits of such claims. This section focuses on analyses of disparity using traditional applicant flow data, and we present both statistical significance tests such as Fisher's exact test and practical significance tests including the four-fifths rule. To better illustrate the use and interpretation of these analytical strategies, we present results with simulated data that include a dichotomous

New Directions for Institutional Research, no. 138, Summer 2008 © Wiley Periodicals, Inc.
Published online in Wiley InterScience (www.interscience.wiley.com) • DOI: 10.1002/ir.248

employment outcome (for example, being promoted or not promoted) and two groups (such as men and women). We conclude with a consideration of the quality of analyses and present issues related to sample size, violations of statistical assumptions, and various characteristics of employment decisions.

It is important to emphasize that the issues covered in this chapter assume accurate and reliable data for analysis, and it can take substantial time and effort to develop and maintain an adequate database. For this reason, readers may find this chapter easier to understand if they have read Chapter 4 on the organization and maintenance of data in employment litigation. In addition, this chapter focuses on the analysis of categorical outcomes such that occur in employment decisions as opposed to continuous outcomes such as pay. For readers who may not be entirely familiar with this distinction, we recommend reading this chapter along with the next chapter, which examines multiple regression analysis in employment litigation.

A Review of Employment Discrimination Litigation

Employment discrimination litigation may involve a variety of employment outcomes. In considering these outcomes, it is useful to review Title VII of the Civil Rights Act of 1964 (as amended by the Civil Rights Act of 1991), which protects individuals against employment discrimination based on race, color, religion, sex, and national origin. This statute makes it illegal for employers to fail or refuse to hire or to discharge any individual, or otherwise to discriminate against any individual with respect to his compensation, terms, conditions, or privileges of employment. . . . or to limit, segregate, or classify his employees or applicants for employment in any way which would deprive or tend to deprive any individual of employment opportunities or otherwise adversely affect his status as an employee.

More traditional bottom-line employment outcomes that have clear financial consequences, such as being selected into an organization, promoted to a higher position, compensated, or fired, are obviously covered by this statute. Importantly, outcomes less financial in nature are also generally covered in the phrase *terms, conditions,* or *privileges* of employment and may include training opportunities, performance appraisal, nontraditional work schedules, and most employee benefits. Executive Order 11246, which implemented mandatory affirmative action for federal contractors in 1965, mirrors the practices covered and protected classes of Title VII, with particular emphasis on previously disadvantaged groups like women and minorities.

All of these types of employment outcomes are protected for individuals forty years of age or older under the Age Discrimination in Employment Act and for disabled individuals under the Americans with Disabilities Act of 1990. Individuals may also be covered under various state statutes, and by older federal statutes including the Rehabilitation Act of 1973, an impor-

NEW DIRECTIONS FOR INSTITUTIONAL RESEARCH • DOI: 10.1002/ir

tant precursor to the Americans with Disabilities Act, and the Equal Pay Act, which covers women against compensation discrimination. In short, the U.S. government intended for all individuals of socially valued group membership to be covered by at least one statute. Enforcement agencies such as the Equal Employment Opportunity Commission and the Office of Federal Contract Compliance Programs (OFCCP) enforce various statutes with the goal of minimizing discrimination in the workplace.

Statistical analyses can be used to examine claims of discrimination under all of these statutes. At a general level, these analyses test the relation between a protected class variable, usually dichotomous, and an employment outcome, which is also often dichotomous. In these situations, the members of the protected class are often referred to as the focal group; members of the comparison group are often referred to as the referent group. The purpose of most analyses is to determine whether a relation exists between protected class membership and the employment outcome of interest. If there is a relation and this relation adversely affects the focal group at or above a socially or scientifically derived criterion, an enforcement agency or court may conclude that discrimination occurred. Statistical analyses help to answer whether members of both groups selected are at similar rates. In cases where selection rates are not equal, the disparity may be evidence of discrimination. From a scientific perspective, this disparity may be statistically significant, which supports the notion that the disparity did not occur by chance. From a socially derived perspective, this disparity may be practically significant, suggesting that the disparity is large enough for an enforcement agency or court to notice.

Categorical Variables

It is important to consider the type of outcome variables considered in the analysis of employment discrimination litigation. The outcomes we are focusing on in this chapter are categorical in nature and, as such, can take on only a small number of values. In addition, there is no real quantitative meaning to the intervals between the values of these categories because choosing a label for a category is somewhat arbitrary. For example, in analyzing a dichotomy such as whether a candidate was promoted, a variable is often dummy-coded as 0 for not being promoted and 1 for being promoted. This dummy code has some attractive statistical properties for the purposes of interpreting analyses. The interval between 0 and 1 has no inherent meaning in a dummy coding scheme. In contrast, continuous variables can usually take on many values, often have a 0 point representing the complete absence of something, and have intervals between values that are inherently meaningful (Agresti, 2002). For example, employee pay, which is discussed in the next chapter, is a continuous outcome that may take on many values, has a 0 point representing the absence of pay, and can be interpreted along a meaningful interval scale such as dollars.

When the outcome of interest is categorical in nature, traditional techniques used to analyze continuous outcomes violate some important statistical assumptions. For example, the assumptions of equal error variance across categories and of normally distributed error terms may be violated when an outcome has only two categories (Allison, 1999; Tabachnick and Fidell, 2001). Both of these assumptions are inherent in the nature of dichotomous outcomes. The consequences of these violations may include inefficient and nonsensical variable relations, attenuated standard errors, and, perhaps most important, a significantly increased chance of finding a statistically significant relation when the significance was due to random chance (also referred to as type I error). Fortunately, a series of categorical data analytic techniques is available for appropriately modeling the relation between a protected class variable and a categorical outcome.

Analyses of Traditional Applicant Flow Data

Given the substantial statutes, regulations, and case law relating to when employment decisions may be considered discriminatory, we now turn to how a researcher may investigate specific personnel practices for evidence relating to potential discrimination. In many cases, the data that are most central to determining whether personnel actions are enacted in a consistent manner across groups are the number of people who apply and are accepted from each group. These data are referred to as applicant flow data. When these data are indicative of the actual application rate to an open position or a series of openings, analysis of these data is the most informative with respect to the consistency of personnel actions across groups. Under these circumstances, they reflect the actual rates at which members of each group apply for a position, are offered a position, and are selected and placed into a position or passed on to the next step in the selection process. For analyses of applicant flow data to be accurate, several conditions must be met. Furthermore, interpretations of the results of these analyses must be tempered by consideration of both statistical and practical significance. This section discusses the conditions under which applicant flow analyses are most useful for analyzing whether there are statistical disparities associated with a selection procedure, the proper methods for analyzing such a disparity, how to determine whether the test has a statistically significant result, and, where there are statistically significant results, whether the disparity is practically significant.

Situations Where Applicant Flow Analyses Are Possible. Proper analysis of applicant flow data requires several conditions to be met: a clearly definable means of entry into the applicant pool, a clearly defined outcome of the selection procedure, separability of the process from other personnel procedures, clearly definable groups of interest, and available records of decisions made as part of the personnel process. These are minimal conditions and do not confer validity on the inferences drawn from such analyses. (Conditions that influence the validity of these analyses are discussed later in this chapter.)

Most critical to determining whether applicant flow analyses are possible is the ability to discern when an individual from the available labor pool has entered into the applicant pool for a particular position. In some cases, these data are not possible or do not include individuals who are the most likely to get a particular position. For example, an internal promotion may have an organizational requirement to be publicly posted for a specified amount of time before an internal candidate may be awarded the position. In these cases, the relevant applicant pool is actually all eligible internal staff, although some cursory consideration is given to external applicants as a procedural matter. In these cases, it may not be clear who was actually considered for the position: external candidates are certainly considered, but not as thoroughly as internal staff who are eligible and interested. The complicating factor is determining which eligible internal candidates are interested in the position. In situations where interest in a promotion must be assumed, traditional applicant flow analyses may not be appropriate, and something more similar to a survival analysis is more appropriate. In these cases, the question changes slightly from whether applicants are promoted at the same rate to how long the average member of each group takes to get promoted.

It is also critical to have a clearly defined outcome of the selection process, such as being passed on to the next step in the selection process or ultimately selected for the position. In situations where the outcome of the process may be indeterminable for some time, such as being rank-ordered with other candidates and put on a waiting list, applicant flow analyses may not be appropriate. Likewise, these outcomes must be separable from other steps in the selection process in the sense that it is clear when one step in the selection process ends and another begins. Separability is not a stringent requirement of applicant flow analysis, but it is helpful in determining what aspect of the selection process may be responsible for differential selection rates (see the discussion of *Connecticut* v. *Teal,* 1982, later in this chapter). Specifically, ideal data for applicant flow analysis are created when each step in the process passes a specific, identifiable set of candidates to the next step in the process, which forms the candidate pool for that next step, and others are excluded from consideration at this point. In cases where candidates may be passed on to the next step with recommendations, rankings, or other nonbinding evaluations, it usually precludes interpretation of these evaluations in an applicant flow analysis.

Another requirement is having clearly definable groups in the applicant pool. To the extent that applicant groups are not well defined, traditional applicant flow analyses are not feasible. For example, some cases refer to disparate impact based on violating gender or ethnic stereotypes, skin tone, or other hard-to-categorize characteristics. If applicants cannot be clearly split into distinct groups, the value of any analysis can be called into question.

NEW DIRECTIONS FOR INSTITUTIONAL RESEARCH • DOI: 10.1002/ir

Finally, accurate record keeping is essential for valid and reliable applicant flow analyses. If records are missing, accurate group information cannot be determined, or it is difficult to tell what happened with a particular application, applicant flow analyses may be affected. The Uniform Guidelines on Employee Selection Procedures (1978), a commonly referenced technical authority on the legal requirements of employment testing, requires all organizations to keep information about the demographic characteristics of applicants and those hired who constitute at least 2 percent of the relevant labor market (Gatewood and Field, 2001). In addition, the OFCCP recently advocated a new set of record-keeping rules in its definition of an Internet applicant.[1] Organizations should adhere to these record-keeping policies because such information is used in both practical and statistical tests of adverse impact.

Analysis of a 2 × 2 Contingency Table. To begin a discussion of a traditional applicant flow analysis, we must revisit the specifications from the previous section. From the criteria specified in that discussion, it should be apparent that applicant flow analyses consist of a series of 2 × 2 contingency tables. That is, the rows of the table typically correspond to two clearly definable applicant groups, and the columns typically correspond to the outcomes of the step in the selection process. Table 5.1 presents a 2 × 2 contingency table that will be used throughout the remainder of this chapter.

Table 5.1 shows the number of people who applied and were accepted and rejected, broken down by gender. In the table, we see that of the ten men who applied for the promotion, nine were accepted. Of the ten women who applied, six were accepted. In this case, the acceptance rate for men (9/10 = 90 percent) is higher than the acceptance rate for women (6/10 = 60 percent). What is not clear is whether this difference is enough to suggest that the process might be discriminatory. The remainder of this section describes the considerations one needs to take into account when examining data such as these.

A key consideration in the analysis of employment decisions is that in almost all cases, the data are observational and retrospective data (Steel, 1990). That is, since the researcher cannot randomly assign individuals to groups, the study is an observational research design as opposed to experimental. Furthermore, the data are retrospective in the sense that the researcher typically does not expect any additional data to become avail-

Table 5.1. Example of a 2 × 2 Contingency Table

	Rejected	Accepted	Total
Men (referent)	1 (RR)	9 (AR)	10 (TR)
Women (focal)	4 (RF)	6 (AF)	10 (TF)
Total	5 (T_{Rej})	15 (T_{Acc})	20 (T_{App})

NEW DIRECTIONS FOR INSTITUTIONAL RESEARCH • DOI: 10.1002/ir

able and usually does not intend to generalize these results to a larger population. A notable exception is when a researcher is conducting an analysis to determine the potential for adverse impact in the future. In other words, the data are what they are, and as such, inferential analysis based on experimental or population sampling models (where it is assumed that the representation of applicants and the number of selections are free to vary) may not be appropriate. Some researchers have taken this concept to an extreme (see Meier, Sacks, and Zabell, 1984, for a discussion of the merits and flaws of this perspective), suggesting that all inferential statistics are inappropriate for retrospective analysis of employment litigation; others argue that there is still utility in statistical significance testing in these situations.

Perhaps the most widely endorsed perspective on analyzing employment decisions is that they must be treated as observational studies using retrospective data. Observational studies are those in which the researcher has no control over the assignment of individuals in the study to treatment groups or, in this case, to the focal or referent group. Clearly it is impossible for a researcher to assign individuals to be men or women; they apply at the rates at which they apply, and the researcher can do nothing to change those rates. Furthermore, the data are retrospective, meaning that the researcher has no influence on the overall passing rate for the step. In some cases, changing a cutoff for being qualified, accepted, or hired might influence the differences in rates at which members of the focal and referent groups are hired. In retrospective analyses, these rates are fixed.

Fisher's Exact Test and Approximations. When data are essentially fixed, most statisticians agree that the proper statistical test for the 2×2 contingency table with fixed margins is Fisher's exact test, a nonparametric statistic (Siskin and Trippi, 2005; Yates, 1984). Although many statisticians have argued that in cases where the margins are not fixed (Upton, 1982; D'Agostino, Chase, and Belanger, 1988), Yates (1984) soundly refutes these arguments, and its accompanying rejoinders by many of the critics of Fisher's exact test note that it is almost certainly appropriate in cases where the data are retrospective or observational in nature and that all other tests are less computationally intensive estimations of the exact test.

Returning to Table 5.1, we can demonstrate how Fisher's exact test can be applied to these data to examine whether the selection procedure in question may be discriminatory. Recall that the overall acceptance rate for men was nine of ten applicants, which resulted in an acceptance rate of 90 percent. For women, only six of ten were accepted, resulting in an acceptance rate of 60 percent. If the 2×2 table is used, the exact probability that the observed acceptance rates would have occurred if applicants from each group were selected at random is expressed using Fisher's formula:

$$p = \binom{TR}{AR}\binom{TF}{AF} \Big/ \binom{TApp}{TAcc},$$

where TR = total referent group members, AR = number of accepted referent group members, TF = total focal group members, AF = number of accepted focal group members, T_{App} = total applicants, and T_{Acc} = total applicants accepted.

This formula simplifies to:

$$p = \frac{TR!\,TF!\,T_{acc}!\,T_{rej}!}{T_{app}!\,AF!\,AR!\,RF!\,RR!},$$

where T_{rej} = the total number of applicants rejected, RF = the number of rejected focal group members, and RR = the number of rejected referent group members.

The previous formula gives the exact probability for a single combination of men and women selected from the pools given a fixed number of selections.[2] For Table 5.1, the probability that exactly nine men were chosen out of the fifteen selections is 0.1354.[3] If we are trying to determine whether this outcome indicates potential discrimination against women applicants, we also need to account for any combination that results in fewer women being selected. In this case, fewer women are selected only if all ten men were selected. Applying the Fisher's exact calculation to a table with five women selected and ten men selected results in a probability of 0.0163. One may continue to sum Fisher's exact test probabilities until either the number of selections is exhausted or the number of focal group selections is zero. Thus, the total probability that 1 or fewer women were selected, if selections were made at random (in other words, without respect to gender), is 0.1354 + 0.0163 = 0.1517. It is common practice to convert this probability to its corresponding Z value based on the normal distribution, as courts often prefer to interpret statistical analyses in terms of normal standard deviations. Statistical results across multiple independent pools can be combined through convolving them into a single result.[4] Note that Fisher's test and other exact statistics can be computationally intensive, and in circumstances with large sample sizes, statistical approximations like the Mantel-Haenzsel test may be used.

The disparity is another value that indicates the magnitude of the shortfall in selections. The disparity is the actual number of selected focal group members less the expected number of selections (the total focal group applicants times the total selected divided by the total number of applicants) from the focal group. Thus, the formula to calculate disparity is:

$$disp_{foc} = AF - TF * \left(\frac{T_{acc}}{T_{app}}\right).$$

For Table 5.1, six of ten women were accepted of ten total women. Fifteen of all twenty applicants were accepted. Thus, we would expect 7.5 of the women to be accepted if the process operated at random, resulting in a disparity of −1.5 women accepted.

NEW DIRECTIONS FOR INSTITUTIONAL RESEARCH • DOI: 10.1002/ir

Statistical Significance. A reasonable question arises as to whether the result of a Fisher's exact test may be considered statistically significant. In this case, significance concerns whether results occurred by chance. Scientific convention typically uses a criterion of $p < .05$ (or $p < .01$ in stricter cases) as the threshold for determining whether a finding can be considered significant (Hays, 1994; Murphy and Myors, 2004). This criterion means that an event must occur less than 5 percent of the time if the process operated at random in order to indicate a reliable difference in the selection rate between the two groups. These statistics are often transformed into a standard deviation metric, where the cut point for statistical significance is often 1.96, corresponding to a p-value of less than or equal to .05, or greater than two (or three) standard deviations (see *Hazelwood School District v. United States*, 1977). The probability of observing results similar to those presented in Table 5.1 is 0.1517, which is greater than 0.05. Therefore, we would conclude that the acceptance rate for women does not statistically differ from that for men.

In most cases, we use a slightly more conservative criterion. In cases where we do not have strong, preexisting evidence that there is a reliable association between two variables in one direction, we split the significance level across the probability that men are selected at a higher rate than women and that women are selected at a higher rate than men. Splitting the significance level across both potential hypotheses is known as *two-tailed* hypothesis testing. Two-tailed hypothesis testing seems to be consistent with the standards used in many significant court rulings (Feinberg, 1989), as well as the publications requirements for many peer-reviewed journals, where editors have become more skeptical of one-tailed hypothesis tests over the years. However, there may be some situations where a one-tailed test is appropriate. For example, if the statistical test is a low power test (see Murphy and Myors, 2004, for a review of statistical power) and there is some additional evidence to suggest discrimination had occurred, such as strong evidence of past discrimination or the equivalent of a smoking gun (for example, an e-mail or public statement made by hiring personnel disparaging members of a particular group), a one-tailed test may be reasonable. This situation might be more comparable to social science applications where one-tailed significance testing is considered appropriate.

Because the results from the previous tests could reflect either unequal treatment or unequal qualifications of applicants, one requirement of this kind of hypothesis testing applied to employment decisions is that all applicants must be similarly situated. Often it is common practice to assume applicants are similarly situated in applicant flow data when they are considered for the same job opening at the same time or within a very short period. For example, if applicants apply to a specific opening, it can generally be assumed that they are similarly situated. In cases where applicant pools are not easily identified, there may be other ways to identify similarly situated applicants. Gilmartin (1991) notes that determining whether applicants are similarly situated can be done by examining relative qualifications or reviewing the composition of the workforce at the time of selection or over a period of time.

Even when applicant pools are well defined, there may be important differences within pools that prevent applicants from being similarly situated. For example, internal applicants generally have a better chance of being hired as compared with external candidates because selecting officials are familiar with their work. Considering these subgroups within the applicant pool to be equivalent in terms of their probability of being selected can provide misleading results unless members of the focal and referent group are equally represented in important subgroups. Subpooling applicant pools is one way to account for important differences in background characteristics or qualifications that may have an important influence on the probability of selection. These pools can be combined later through convolving each separate pool into a single pool. Another approach that could be used is to remove the effects of background characteristics through the use of logistic regression analysis.

A final consideration is who should be in the comparison group. In some cases, the complaint may include specific language about the referent group, for example, "women received fewer promotions as compared with men." In contrast, the Uniform Guidelines on Employee Selection Procedures (1978) suggests using the most favored group, which often results in an appropriate test. Three issues should be considered before using the most favored group. First, using the most favored group may result in a much lower sample size than using the largest applicant group or all other applicant groups combined. A second and related issue is that the most favored group, if derived empirically, might bias the statistical test toward more phase Type I alpha errors. Third, when discrimination is present, the disparity no longer always represents the number of selections that might be an appropriate remedy. For example, if a third group is also subject to the discrimination when compared to the favored group, it might be appropriate to award some or all of the disparity to the third group as a remedy.

Adverse Impact Ratio and Four-Fifths Rule. Even when the analysis of employment decision results in a finding of a statistically significant disparity, the results do not always indicate unlawful discrimination. One criticism of statistical tests of significance is that there is no intuitive practical significance metric for interpretation, and even trivial differences in selection rates result in statistically significant findings with large sample sizes. The Uniform Guidelines on Employee Selection Procedures state that for an employment practice to be considered discriminatory, it must result in members of the focal group being selected at less than four-fifths (or 80 percent) of the rate of the referent group. The statistic, called the adverse impact ratio, is calculated by dividing the proportion of focal group selections by the proportion of referent group selections.

NEW DIRECTIONS FOR INSTITUTIONAL RESEARCH • DOI: 10.1002/ir

Both the scientific community and the courts are split on the use of this rule, alternatively called the four-fifths rule or the 80 percent rule. The scientific community often balks at the 80 percent rule because the test may be conducted without regard to sampling error. When sample sizes are small, the 80 percent rule is often violated due to sampling error rather than actual adverse impact against the referent group. Courts are inconsistent with respect to their use of the 80 percent rule. Meier, Sacks, and Zabell (1984) note that the Supreme Court has given at least its implicit endorsement to the 80 percent rule in *Connecticut* v. *Teal,* but the use of the "two to three standard deviations" rule cited in *Castaneda* v. *Partida* (1977) explicitly in other decisions (see also King, 2007).

In Table 5.1, we see that the acceptance rate for women is six out of ten (.6), whereas the acceptance rate for men is nine out of ten (.9). The adverse impact ratio for this applicant pool would be .667 (.6/.9), which would indicate that women are accepted at 66.7 percent of the rate at which men are accepted. Although this violates the 80 percent rule, it is not a statistically significant finding. Thus, these data are somewhat equivocal as to whether the selection process in question results in adverse impact toward women because the two different detection methods lead to different conclusions.

One interesting hybrid method of adverse impact detection, proposed by Morris and Lobsenz (2000), is to compute confidence intervals around the adverse impact ratio, which combines both practical and statistical significance testing. This method is attractive because the adverse impact ratio, an estimate of practical significance, can be assessed using a statistical significance test and may or may not contain the four-fifths point on the continuum. However, we are not aware of this methodology being endorsed by a court or enforcement agency. Clearly more evidence is needed to resolve this issue from both a scientific and a legal perspective.

Issues Influencing the Appropriateness of Applicant Flow Data

We now discuss several issues that can affect the appropriateness of applicant flow data: sample size, statistical power, frequent applicants, and withdrawals.

Sample Size and Statistical Power. Statistical power is broadly defined as the probability that a statistical significance test will correctly reject a false null hypothesis. In the case of disparity analyses, the null hypothesis is that there is no difference in selection rates between the focal and referent groups. Disparity analysis is thus contingent on the power of the employed statistical tests. A statistical test with high power has a high probability of detecting any disparity, if in fact it really exists. And a statistical test with low power has a low probability of detecting any disparity, if in fact it exists.

New Directions for Institutional Research • DOI: 10.1002/ir

Several factors can bear on the power of a disparity analysis (Biddle, 2001): effect size, the alpha level (probability of type I error), type of employed statistical test, and sample size (Cohen, 1992). In discrimination analysis, the effect size often refers to the selection rates of the protected groups. Larger differences in selection rates are associated with higher power as compared to smaller effect sizes. Using a one-tailed test or increasing the alpha level also increases the power of an analysis. In addition, tests including Fisher's exact test are generally more powerful as compared to approximations like the Mantel-Haenszel statistic, especially with small samples. With regard to sample size, smaller samples produce less precise results, and standard errors are associated with smaller values of the test statistic required in order to obtain statistical significance. With larger samples, smaller effect sizes can be found to be significantly different because there is more precision in the analysis. Subgroup sample sizes also play a role in the power of the statistical analysis. When the focal group makes up a small percentage of the total sample, statistical significance tests need to be heeded. For instance, when a sample is composed of 95 percent referent class members and 5 percent focal class members, flipping one focal class member outcome from rejected to selected can drastically change results.

Note that organizations generally have little control over the effect size in disparity analyses. In addition, enforcement agencies and courts usually prefer a two-tailed significance test with an alpha level equal to 0.05, so organizations have little control over evaluation criteria as well. The type of statistical test is, however, under the control of the researcher. Because exact tests are more powerful as compared to estimator tests, they are preferred. In addition, organizations may be able to increase the size of the sample, thus increasing the power of the analysis. Biddle (2001) recommends the following methods to increase the analyzed sample size: widening the time frame of the analysis, combining geographical regions, and combining jobs into an overall adverse impact analysis, as detailed above. However, when retrospective data are used, the researcher may not be able to increase the sample size. Also consider the notion of overpowering a statistical test: in some cases, extremely large samples may produce a statistically significant result simply because of the sample size. As such, organizations should consider both statistical and practical estimates of significance to determine the magnitude of disparity.

Unfortunately, the courts have provided little guidance on minimum sample size requirements for conducting discrimination analyses. Typically the courts view such requirements on a case-by-case basis (Biddle, 2001). The Uniform Guidelines do provide some guidance on the matter, stating that when significant results are based on samples that are too small to be reliable, the researcher should attempt to lengthen the time period analyzed in an attempt to obtain a larger sample. Furthermore, the Uniform Guidelines recommend that when small samples are the basis of the analysis, evidence pertaining to similar selection systems should be obtained and used to support or refute discrimination.

Frequent Applicants. As automated recruitment and selection systems have eased the time, effort, and expense an applicant must put forth to file an application, the likelihood an applicant submits applications to multiple vacancies within an organization has increased. This possibility may be even greater in large organizations with a high number of diverse jobs, where a high level of effort is required for creating and submitting a single job application, but little additional effort is required to extend that existing submission to other jobs. Applicants who apply to multiple vacancies may influence the observed disparity associated with a selection step, as the assumption of independence is violated.

Statistical significance tests such as Fisher's exact test generally require that the assumption of independent observations is met. Broadly defined, *independent* means that the results in one pool give no information about what was likely to happen in another pool. When the observations are covariant (not independent), as is the case when a single applicant files multiple applications, the statistical analyses may be affected. From a statistical perspective, covariant observations represent a confounding source of systematic variance attributed to the applicant, and, thus, not to the protected group of interest. From an applied perspective, dependent observations may influence whether the magnitude of a disparity does (if the frequent applier is a member of the focal group) or does not (if the frequent applier is from the referent group) achieve statistical and practical significance criteria.

To the extent that independence does not hold, the analysis may overestimate the statistical significance of any disparities. For example, suppose there are five different but similar positions available and the same 20 people (10 men and 10 women) apply for all five; 15 applicants (9 men and 6 women) are selected. If this is analyzed as a single set of selections, the expected number of women to pass this first hurdle is 7.5, so the disparity is -1.5; the z value from Fisher's exact test is -1.03 and not statistically significant. In contrast, if the same results are used five times and are analyzed as though five pools are independent, the expected number of women to pass this step is 37.5 (five times as large), the disparity is -7.5 (five times as large), and the z value is -3.23, which is beyond the value required for statistical significance.

A more realistic example is the case where the twenty applicants are evaluated by five different interviewers for five different but similar positions. In this example, knowing which applicants passed the first hurdle for one position no longer provides perfect information about which applicants will pass the first hurdle for the other positions. However, it does provide some information because of the expectation that those who passed the first position hurdle are more likely to pass the first hurdle for the other positions. This situation is a violation of the assumption of independence and tends to make any disparities (in either direction) larger than they should be. The extent of the problem is not easy to quantify.

Interpretation of disparity analyses in the presence of frequent appliers is challenging. For example, the treatment typical group members receive might not be the same as the treatment received by a frequent applier in that group, and a significant disparity might be due to one individual. Given this issue, researchers and practitioners may need to identify frequent appliers and determine their aggregate influence on the statistical test performed. Such identification can occur along a number of dimensions: number of submitted applications compared to the average number of submitted applications, number of vacancies that the applicant is deemed unqualified, and computing cumulative disparity associated with an applicant across all pools. Once criteria to identify frequent appliers have been established, the handling of such applications needs to be determined. Currently, there is little guidance or case law concerning the handling of frequent appliers in adverse impact analyses.[5] Such treatment may include keeping these applications in the analyses, eliminating these applications from the analyses, excluding only those applications deemed unqualified, or modeling qualification measures to account for this issue using logistic regression analyses.

Withdrawals. A related issue concerns treatment of applicant and organizational withdrawals in analyses. Usually, at any point in a selection system, applicants may withdraw from consideration or indicate a lack of interest in a job. For example, an applicant may have been offered another job, may no longer want to be considered for employment, and may actively withdraw from consideration. In any selection system, the treatment of such individuals must be considered because the inclusion or exclusion of withdrawals may influence disparity results. That is, at what point in the selection system should such withdrawals be eliminated from the analysis? Assuming there is agreement to remove withdrawals from analysis, there are generally two options. First, one could include such applicants in the analysis for all steps prior to their withdrawal. For instance, an applicant passes a written test, passes a phone interview, and is invited for an in-person interview but withdraws from consideration at this step. Such an applicant would be included in the analysis for the first two steps but omitted from any analysis of subsequent steps. Second, one could exclude such applicants from all the steps in the analysis. In other words, such a person was never an actual applicant and would not be included in any of the analyses of the individual steps.

The courts have provided little guidance in the matter of how to treat such withdrawals. Logical arguments can be made for both cases. Inclusion of applicants in the steps they completed is reasonable because at the time of the step, the applicant may have truly been considering the vacancy. This also increases the sample size of the analysis of the particular step. Alternatively, one can also consider whether withdrawals truly ever consider the position as a viable choice. Some situations, such as federal civil service positions, require the applicant to list all jobs that he or she would like to be considered for. However, such an applicant may be pulled for a job opening that he or she did not truly intend to be pulled for and pass one or more of the steps in the selection system without any action on his or her part (including meeting experience and education requirements, considered basically qualified, and so on). However, when this person is notified of being considered for such a position, the applicant may withdraw from the competition, as he or she had no intent for obtaining such an opening. In this instance, it seems reasonable that such applicants should be omitted from the analysis. Also note that the organization may withdraw a job opening for various reasons, such as a hiring freeze. In these cases, applicant pools should not be included in adverse impact analyses.

Conclusion

The purpose of this chapter has been to describe how employment outcomes can be analyzed in employment discrimination litigation. Toward that end, we introduced the legal context around making employment decisions. We next presented a series of categorical data analyses that are generally appropriate for analyzing those decisions for disparity. We considered a variety of important factors that may affect the implications of these analyses, which are often critical in determining the admissibility of results in case preparation, trial, and settlement.

In our opinion, the issue of discrimination in employment selection will only become more important with the development of employment selection procedures that use the Internet and other automated systems as applicant pool formation techniques. Although the ability to create an applicant pool has become substantially easier in recent years, the requirement of making employment decisions that are job related and nondiscriminatory has not. Being familiar with the issues presented in this chapter should help readers better understand employment discrimination claims, what are proper and improper data and analyses regarding these claims, and how such analyses are used in litigation.

Notes

1. http://www.dol.gov/esa/regs/compliance/ofccp/faqs/iappfaqs.htm.

2. Some readers may be familiar with the traditional chi-square tests used to approximate Fisher's exact test. However, traditional chi squares are typically inaccurate for small samples in 2×2 tables (for example, when the expected value of a cell is 5 or less). In addition, the hypergeometric distribution is used instead of the binomial distribution because applicants typically are selected from the pool without replacement.

3. For the exact probability of nine referent selections from fifteen total selections, $p = 0.1354$.

4. Fully describing the process of convolving across multiple pools would require too much space to do so adequately within the scope of this chapter. In short, the process involves summing the joint probability of all combinations that focal group members selected (from zero to the total across both pools). This process is described well in Palmer and McLaughlin (1990). For Table 5.1, convolving across two pools would result in a probability of 0.023, which would be significant.

5. One recent possible exception is the OFCCP Systemic Compensation Discrimination Standards and Voluntary Guidelines for Compensation Self-Evaluation, which suggests removing "influential cases" in some instances. A summary of these standards can be found at http://www.dol.gov/esa/regs/compliance/ofccp/faqs/comstrds.htm.

References

Agresti, A. *Categorical Data Analysis*. Hoboken, N.J.: Wiley, 2002.

Allison, P. *Logistic Regression Using the SAS System: Theory and Application*. Cary, N.C.: SAS Institute, 1999.

Biddle, D. *Adverse Impact and Test Validation: A Practitioner's Guide to Valid and Defensible Employment Testing*. (2nd ed.) Burlington, Vt.: Gower Publishing, 2001.

Castaneda v. Partida, 430 U.S. 482 (1977).

Cohen, J. "A Power Primer." *Psychological Bulletin*, 1992, *1*, 155–159.

Connecticut v. Teal, 457 U.S. 440 (1982).

D'Agostino, R., Chase, W., and Belanger, A. "The Appropriateness of Some Common Procedures for Testing the Equality of Two Independent Binomial Populations." *American Statistician*, 1988, *42*, 198–202.

Feinberg, S. (ed.). *The Evolving Role of Statistical Assessments as Evidence in Courts*. New York: Springer-Verlag, 1989.

Gatewood, R., and Field, H. *Human Resource Selection*. (5th ed.) Orlando, Fla.: Harcourt, 2001.

Gilmartin, K. "Identifying Similarly Situated Employees in Employment Discrimination Cases." *Jurimetrics Journal*, 1991, *31*(4), 429–440.

Hays, W. *Statistics*. (5th ed.) Orlando, Fla.: Harcourt, 1994.

Hazelwood School District v. United States, 433 U.S. 299.31 n. 17 (1977).

King, A. "'Gross Statistical Disparities' as Evidence of a Pattern and Practice of Discrimination: Statistical Versus Legal Significance." *Labor Lawyer*, 2007, *22*, 271–292.

Meier, P., Sacks, J., and Zabell, S. "What Happened in *Hazelwood*: Statistics, Employment Discrimination, and the 80% Rule." *American Bar Foundation Research Journal*, 1984, *1*, 139–186.

Morris, S., and Lobsenz, R. "Significance Tests and Confidence Intervals for the Adverse Impact Ratio." *Personnel Psychology*, 2000, *53*, 89–112.

Murphy, K., and Myors, B. *Statistical Power Analysis: A Simple and General Model for Traditional and Modern Hypothesis Tests*. (2nd ed.) Mahwah, N.J.: Erlbaum, 2004.

Palmer, C., and McLaughlin, D. "The Analysis of Selection Events." In K. Gilmartin and others (eds.), *Application of Statistical Methods to the Analysis of Employment Data: A Guide to the Use of Statistics in the Adjudication of Discrimination Claims*. Washington, D.C.: American Institutes for Research, 1990.

Siskin, B., and Trippi, J. "Statistical Issues in Employment Litigation." In F. Landy (ed.), *Employment Discrimination Litigation: Behavioral, Quantitative, and Legal Perspectives*. San Francisco: Jossey-Bass, 2005.

Steel, L. "Observational Studies: Limitations and Constraints." In K. Gilmartin and others (eds.), *Application of Statistical Methods to the Analysis of Employment Data: A Guide to the Use of Statistics in the Adjudication of Discrimination Claims*. Washington, D.C.: American Institutes for Research, 1990.

Tabachnick, B., and Fidell, L. *Using Multivariate Statistics*. Needham Heights, Mass.: Allyn & Bacon, 2001.

Uniform Guidelines on Employee Selection Procedures, 29 C.F.R. sec. 1607 (1978).

Upton, G. "A Comparison of Alternative Tests for the 2 × 2 Comparative Trial." *Journal of the Royal Statistical Society*, 1982, *145*, 86–105.

Yates F. "Tests of Significance for 2 × 2 Contingency Tables." *Journal of the Royal Statistical Society*, 1984, *147*, 426–463.

Zink, D., and Gutman, A. "Statistical Trends in Private Sector Employment Discrimination Suits." In F. Landy (ed.), *Employment Discrimination Litigation: Behavioral, Quantitative, and Legal Perspectives*. San Francisco: Jossey-Bass, 2005.

LORIN M. MUELLER *is a senior research scientist with American Institutes for Research in Washington, D.C.*

ERIC M. DUNLEAVY *is a senior consultant with DCI Consulting Group in Washington, D.C.*

ASH K. BUONASERA *is a senior manager with Marriott International in Bethesda, Maryland.*

6

Through a history of decisions, the courts have outlined how regression models should be used in discrimination cases.

Regression Analysis: Legal Applications in Institutional Research

Julie A. Frizell, Benjamin S. Shippen Jr., Andrew L. Luna

Courts have decided dozens of discrimination cases within higher education over the past twenty years. During this time, increasing attention has been given to inferential statistical investigations, such as regression analyses, to determine liability in these lawsuits, particularly with respect to an institution's pay, hiring, and promotion decisions of its faculty. In this case, regression analysis is used to evaluate the relationship between a set of independent (explanatory) variables with a single, dependent variable. Discrete (dichotomous) decisions within academia, such as hiring and granting tenure, can be analyzed using logistic regression methods; faculty salary, a continuous variable, can be investigated using multiple regression analysis.

This chapter reviews multiple regression analysis, describes how its results should be interpreted, and instructs institutional researchers on how to conduct such analyses using an example focused on faculty pay equity between men and women. The use of multiple regression analysis will be presented as a method with which to compare salaries of male and female faculty in institutional studies or to establish or contest a prima facie case of discrimination in faculty salary equity cases and as a procedure for determining compensation and computing relief during settlement proceedings of faculty pay disparity cases. A brief review of significant case law and court decisions that have defined the role and scope of regression analysis in gender pay disparity cases is also provided. From this review, it will be clear that while statistical analyses are being used by the courts, the various interpretations of these

NEW DIRECTIONS FOR INSTITUTIONAL RESEARCH, no. 138, Summer 2008   © Wiley Periodicals, Inc.
Published online in Wiley InterScience (www.interscience.wiley.com) • DOI: 10.1002/ir.249

analyses are subject to the sometimes incongruence of the rule of law as compared to the science of statistics (Luna, 2006).

The Basic Model

The basic multiple regression model suggests that the continuous variable of salary is dependent on a number of explanatory variables, such as rank, merit, tenure, and any other factor that, according to an institution's faculty pay schedule policy, contributes to the value of a job and therefore affects salary. This relationship can be expressed mathematically as

$$y = a + b_1x_1 + b_2x_2 + \cdots + b_nx_n + e,$$

where a is a numerical constant representing average salary if all other explanatory factors are 0 (for example, a newly hired faculty member who just received her degree and so does not currently have measures of rank, merit, or tenure). The b's are the regression coefficients that represent the size of the relationship between the dependent variable y (salary) with the corresponding explanatory variables x_i where $i = 1, 2, \ldots, n$ (for example, $x_1 =$ rank, $x_2 =$ merit, $x_3 =$ years of tenure) as the amount average salary changes with a one-unit increase in x (an additional year of tenure) when all other variables are controlled. A positive or negative sign on the b coefficient indicates whether salary will increase or decrease with an increase in the corresponding x. The residual error, e, is the random factor that captures random chance and every influence on salary that has not been controlled for in the model (perhaps for a hard-to-quantify characteristic such as dedication). Residual error is defined to be deviations of observations from their expected values as predicted by the model; here, the error term is predicted salary less actual observed salary.

The a and b's from the equation are estimated based on university data collected on the sample of faculty members who are being analyzed, and these coefficients are used to generate a regression line. The most frequently used measure of how good a fit the regression line is to observed salaries is the minimum sum of squared residuals or the coefficients that minimize the sum of squared errors.

The measure of how accurate the regression model is in predicting salaries for faculty included in the analysis is the coefficient of determination, or R^2. This statistic is the proportion of the variance in salary that is explained collectively by the variance of the explanatory variables included in the regression model. R^2 ranges from 0 percent, indicating no linear relationship exists between the explanatory variables and salary, to 100 percent, signifying salary can be predicted perfectly by the explanatory variables in the model. Hence, the higher the R^2 value, the more accurate the regression model because the sum of the squared residuals is reduced. Adding explanatory variables to a regression model will almost always produce a higher

NEW DIRECTIONS FOR INSTITUTIONAL RESEARCH • DOI: 10.1002/ir

value of R^2 regardless of whether these additional variables are themselves statistically significant predictors of salary. This increased value is due to the chance relations between the additional variables and the unexplained variance. Therefore, R^2 is typically adjusted to account for the number of explanatory variables and the number of observations being analyzed.

The analyst must make a number of decisions and a set of key assumptions that should be met to generate stable and reliable multiple regression results for sufficiently large samples in a faculty salary equity study or analysis. First, the analyst must decide who to include in the population sample to be modeled. Within the academic literature, this question generates varied responses as to whether administrators, medical faculty, part-time, adjunct, temporary, or non-tenure-track faculty should be used since they likely follow different pay structures from most full-time faculty at any institution. Gray (1993) and Hamermesh (1996) warned that by not including part-time, non-tenure-track positions in a salary equity model, a traditional low-paid group of faculty who are disproportionately female will be denied salary corrections if disparities exist. Haignere (2002) also concluded that all faculty should be included in the analysis because the capabilities of regression can account for varying group factors.

Other studies state that the job of full-time faculty is significantly different from that of part-time faculty in terms of teaching and research expectations (Chronister, Ganeneder, Harper, and Baldwin, 1997) and that only full-time faculty should be used in equity studies because too many extraneous factors enter into the analysis and provide inconclusive information about why faculty receive different salaries (Braskamp, Muffo, and Langston, 1978). According to Snyder, Hyer, and McLaughlin (1994), including part-time and temporary faculty presents special problems to the regression analysis, so these faculty members are often left out of salary equity models. When part-time faculty members are included in the analysis, adjustments must be made so that the salaries of full-time and part-time faculty are comparable. The researcher conducting the salary analysis must determine who to include in the model by weighing these arguments against the salary structure policies of the university or college being analyzed.

Second, the model must be correctly specified. The relationship between the dependent and explanatory variables must be linear; otherwise the results will underestimate the true relationship between them. The model should be based on the salary policies relevant to the institution being investigated. All relevant explanatory variables according to that institution's pay structure policy should be included in the model, including rank, merit, tenure, department, performance or productivity, and quality of teaching and research. One difficulty with this approach, however, is that institutional databases may not contain information on some of these measures, particularly those relating to productivity.

The choice of which explanatory variables to use has undergone intense debate throughout the literature. According to Fisher (1980), the wrong predictors can either overestimate or underestimate a regression model and could lead to a violation of the basic assumptions of the analysis. Other literature has been quite specific as to which variables should be used and which should not be considered when conducting a regression analysis on faculty salary. For a fuller discussion of this subject, consult McLaughlin and Howard (2003), Toutkoushian (2002, 2003), Boudreau and others (1997), Balzer and others (1996), Webster (1995), Snyder, Hyer, and McLaughlin (1994), Bohannon (1988), and McLaughlin, Smart, and Montgomery (1978).

Failure to include all important explanatory variables in the model creates an omitted variable bias, which would affect the estimated coefficients for the variables included in the model. (This is discussed in more depth later in this chapter.) Some relevant explanatory variables cannot be directly measured or are hard to quantify, requiring the use of proxy variables or measurable variables that are good substitutes for the immeasurable explanatory variable. For example, a potential proxy for productivity is number of publications. Because this proxy does not take quality of the research or level of peer review into account, the inclusion of additional explanatory proxy variables to control for these factors may be required to correctly model the university's pay process.

Conversely, the inclusion of irrelevant explanatory variables may generate erroneous results if they are correlated with any relevant variables, since the results may be incorrectly attributed to the irrelevant ones. The inclusion of explanatory variables that are affected by an institution's discriminatory behavior, otherwise known as potentially tainted variables, may also underestimate discrimination, if it exists. For example, if performance appraisals conducted by the university are proxies for teaching quality and are used to determine faculty salary levels, then a discriminating university may not be identified as such because the coefficient on appraisals could capture some of the discriminatory effect.

Third, the dependent and explanatory variables must be accurate and should not display highly skewed characteristics or be wrought with substantial outliers that could distort the resulting relationships found. The explanatory variables also should not display excessive correlation among themselves (meaning that they are linear functions of each other), known as multicollinearity. (Later in this chapter we discuss how multicollinearity affects regression results.)

Finally, residual errors associated with different observations are assumed to be uncorrelated or independent. Since the error is the sum of all small factors not already included in the model, some of which have a positive relationship with salary and some a negative relationship, by construction the error term will have a mean of zero. The errors are also assumed to be uncorrelated with each other (*nonautocorrelation*) or with any explanatory variable, and to have the same variance for every combination of explanatory variables (*homoscedasticity*) to ensure that the errors are dis-

NEW DIRECTIONS FOR INSTITUTIONAL RESEARCH • DOI: 10.1002/ir

persed randomly. For more detailed discussions of multiple regression analysis and its assumptions, refer to any introductory econometrics text, such as Gujarati (2003), Kennedy (2003), or Maddala (2001).

Testing for Discrimination

It is a fair assumption that faculty with the same qualifications should receive the same salary in the absence of discrimination. Therefore, if predicted salaries from a correctly specified multiple regression model differ between male and female faculty with the same qualifications, then that is evidence of possible discrimination.

Two basic multiple regression procedures are typically used by statistical testifying experts when establishing or contesting a prima facie case of discrimination in faculty salary equity cases. Both procedures can be used by institutional researchers when testing for faculty pay disparities in their studies. The first is the one-equation method, where a variable representing gender is included as one of the explanatory variables in the regression model. The coefficient on the gender variable can be interpreted as the average overall disparity between male and female faculty salaries; if the gender coefficient shows a statistically significant difference between male and female faculty salaries based on the same characteristics, then the difference is likely not due to random chance and is possibly due to discrimination. This method assumes that all the coefficients for the other explanatory variables are exactly the same for the male and female faculty being compared, and the total disadvantage of being female is represented by the coefficient on the gender variable.

The second procedure is the two-equation method, where regressions are run separately for male faculty and female faculty to determine if each group is treated similarly with respect to pay by the institution. The resulting intercepts and coefficient estimates for males and females are compared from the two models using additional tests to see if they are statistically similar. Finkelstein and Levin (1990) claim that the two-equation model would limit the problems associated with a single-equation model, such as the problem with tainted variables, the omission of important variables, incorrect aggregation of different groups, inclusion of prediscrimination law data, and speculative assumptions that the independent variables are determinant of pay raises and promotions. These authors do add, however, that the major drawback of the two-equation model is the loss of statistical power, because each regression has smaller sample sizes than the one-equation model. There may even be too few observations to estimate coefficients reliably.

Toutkoushian and Hoffman (2002) contend that the single-equation model may be more appealing when dealing with small numbers of faculty or a smaller institution, whereas the multiple-equation methods are better used at larger institutions or when the data involve national and not institutional studies. Most important, these authors recommend using multiple methods in a faculty gender equity study in order to determine if the conclusions reached in each analysis are sensitive to the type of model used. Not only is this suggestion practical for increasing the study's reliability and validity, the procedure of comparing the results from both a single-equation model and a multiple-equation model may be a more pragmatic way of introducing a more complex model to jurists if the matter goes to court.

Violations of Key Assumptions

Under the regular assumptions of multiple regression, the coefficient estimates for the explanatory variables are unbiased, consistent, and efficient. There are two common violations of these assumptions that are of particular importance in the context of testing employment outcomes, such as estimating for potential discrimination in faculty salaries. The first problem is omitted variables, or when the model is underspecified and important explanatory factors that explain the dependent variable are left out of the model. The second problem is multicollinearity, where two or more explanatory variables are too closely related to one another. These problems can be interrelated within the same regression model.

Omitted Variable Bias. Within the omitted variable problem, the variation of the omitted variable is left to be explained by the remaining elements of the model, leading to a host of problems for the estimates of those elements. First, the constant term will likely be biased because it will capture some of the effects of the omitted variable on salary. Next, the errors for the model are no longer pulled from a distribution with a mean variance of zero, so the standard errors for the explanatory variables will be biased. Finally, and perhaps most important, if the omitted variable is correlated with an explanatory variable in the model, the coefficient estimate will be biased, as the common variance between the two factors is reflected in the estimate of the included variable.

These violations are of special concern when estimating pay in the discrimination regression model because each has the potential to render biased coefficients or invalid hypotheses tests for the protected group. It is also important to note that the direction of the bias in the coefficient or standard errors depends on the relationship between the omitted variable and the protected group.

Because it was assumed in this example that women, on average, were more likely than men to have a terminal degree, the omission of a terminal degree variable from the model would bias the coefficient on the gender variable for women in a positive direction and reduce the appearance of a negative disparity, possibly to the point where women appear to be earning a premium (in other words, a positive coefficient on the gender variable). In addition, the standard errors of the gender variable would be increased so the t-statistics for gender would be reduced.

This result creates issues for an institution conducting a faculty pay equity study or for a plaintiff trying to establish a prima facie case of gender discrimination in a faculty pay disparity lawsuit. If discrimination is the reason that female faculty are earning two thousand dollars less than their male counterparts, then the omission of the terminal degree variable from the model will reduce the probability that the model will be able to identify such discrimination, and it may in fact create the false impression that women, on average, are earning more than men.

Notice, however, that the omitted variable effect could also move in the opposite direction. Assume there was no discrimination against women and male faculty had the greater percentage of terminal degrees. Omitting the terminal degree variable in this instance would cause the coefficient on the gender variable for women to be biased toward being more negative than if the terminal degree variable was included. The standard errors would still be larger than if the omitted variable was included, but the larger coefficient on the gender variable for women could appear statistically significant when in the "true" model it should not be under the assumption of no gender discrimination. Clearly, omitted variable bias can be important to both sides in the context of labor and employment discrimination analysis.

Multicollinearity. Multicollinearity occurs when the regression model is close to being overspecified—that is, when two or more variables on the right-hand side of the regression equation are so closely related that they move in almost complete dependence of one another. If the collinear variables move completely in concert, the effect is called perfect collinearity, and the regression model fails because there are not enough degrees of freedom to allow an estimation of the coefficients for the collinear independent variables. The model will allow estimation if there is near perfect collinearity. Such situations can pose problems as well as present opportunities that are worth discussing.

Multicollinearity makes the effect of the correlated explanatory variables impossible to separate, where coefficients on these variables appear too big or too small in relation to their true values while inflating their standard errors. Consider the same example used above but where terminal degree is included in the regression model. The variables for terminal degree and aptitude may be multicollinear. If so, the standard errors for each are going to be larger than they would be in the absence of one of the variables, reducing the t-statistics. No hypothesis test of these explanatory variables is possible in this situation.

However, multicollinearity does not bias the estimation of salary or the coefficients of uncorrelated explanatory variables in the model. Therefore, if multicollinearity occurs between explanatory variables that are not in the model for purposes of direct estimation, such as the gender variable, it may not matter to the analysis. Since it is often more important to fully control for an effect to avoid omitted variable bias, some multicollinearity is acceptable, although including more variables than necessary reduces the adjusted R^2 (explanatory power) of the model. Again consider the example of gender discrimination. The estimates of the terminal degree and aptitude coefficients (and standard errors) are clearly incorrect if they are closely correlated, but

NEW DIRECTIONS FOR INSTITUTIONAL RESEARCH • DOI: 10.1002/ir

it is necessary to fully control for the effects of both a terminal degree and aptitude to avoid omitted variable bias, especially in this case where women faculty are more likely to have a terminal degree and perhaps have higher aptitudes on average than male faculty.

Compensation Determination and Relief Computations

During the liability phase of pay equity cases, the statistical significance of the coefficient on the gender indicator variable in the one-equation regression model determines whether differences in predicted salary of faculty with the same characteristics are due to chance or are possibly due to discrimination. If the court rules that the pay disparities are due to unlawful discrimination by the institution, the next step in the process is to determine compensation and how much relief is required to make the discriminated parties whole (in other words, restore salary levels that would have been reached but for the discrimination).

Once the regression line is determined from the model estimates, actual and predicted salaries can be graphed against the lines to determine which faculty positions are undercompensated or are found below the regression line. How much should the underpaid faculty members be compensated? There are arguments for two different amounts. The first is to subtract actual, observed female faculty salaries from predicted salaries. This brings underpaid individuals up to the average salary as predicted by the model; individuals earning more than predicted are not compensated. An argument against this method is that female faculty who earn more than their predicted salary may be more productive ("star performers"), while those earning less may be less productive ("shirkers"). This method would penalize those star performers and overcompensate the shirkers.

Conversely, the second method subtracts predicted salary for a woman from predicted salary of male faculty with the same characteristics, the difference defined to be pay lost due to gender discrimination (Gilmartin and Hartka, 1991). In this case, even if observed salary is above her predicted salary, a female faculty member would still receive relief because this method does not overweight female faculty members who are less productive than others. Recall that the use of the gender indicator in the one-equation regression model assumes the other coefficients are the same for male and female faculty, so the gender indicator estimates only the difference in average salaries between male and female faculty that is not accounted for by differences in qualifications. Gilmartin and Hartka argue that the analysis should be run under the two-equation method or under one regression but including interaction terms between gender and each of the other explanatory variables to determine whether any additional information can be assessed on which qualification(s) is (are) related to the salary difference. For example, are female faculty paid less because they are not given as much credit for their rank? Each female faculty member would then be paid relief based on her individual case, not the average amount of the pay disparity.

Salary remedies can be applied to correct for all past inequities or simply to remedy current inequities. Total relief required to increase the female faculty earnings up to a level but for the discrimination can be computed individually by predicting the female faculty member's salary for each year that she is employed and summing up over those years the differences between her salary (actual or predicted) and an equivalent male faculty member's salary. Relief can also be computed in a class-wide environment where the coefficient on the gender variable in the one-equation model is multiplied by the number of class members and their total work hours over the liability period; this amount can be redistributed based on which individuals have the largest discrepancies in actual versus predicted wages.

Case Law Review

Two statutes exist on which claims of sex discrimination in employment are filed: the Equal Pay Act and Title VII of the 1964 Civil Rights Act. Currently faculty use both statutes to dispute pay disparities in higher education; however, the Title VII statute is considered the more comprehensive and has become the most frequently used discrimination statute within higher education. Although the Equal Pay Act has been applied to discrimination cases for both men and women, only members of underrepresented or suspect class groups can file a discrimination claim under Title VII. According to the Second Circuit Court, the major difference in the two statutes is that a Title VII disparate treatment claim requires a showing of discriminatory intent, and an Equal Pay Act claim does not.

The U.S. Supreme Court established the basic analytical framework for providing an individual case of intentional discrimination, or disparate treatment, under Title VII. The Court stated that the plaintiff could prove unlawful discrimination, and once the showing has been made, an employer must articulate a legitimate, nondiscriminatory reason in order to avoid liability (*McDonnell Douglas Corp.* v. *Green,* 1973). This decision induced plaintiffs and defendants alike to use statistics as part of their probative evidence. Soon after this decision, courts were obligated to recognize an increase of statistical evidence in discrimination cases. In *Hazelwood School District* v. *U.S.* (1977), the court clarified the use of statistics in Title VII cases by stating that the government could establish a prima facie case of race discrimination by the use of statistics. The U.S. Supreme Court's decision in *International Brotherhood of Teamsters* v. *U.S.* (1977) further confirmed the use of statistics in discrimination cases when it held that statistics are probative of discrimination, especially when they are combined with anecdotal evidence.

Multiple regression analysis has provided more compelling evidence in Title VII cases than in Equal Pay Act claims. In *Houck* v. *Virginia Polytechnic*

Institute and State University (1993), the Fourth Circuit affirmed the lower court's decision when it ruled that the plaintiff failed to compare herself to a particular male comparator. The court noted that she compared herself to a hypothetical male, not one who actually existed. In citing *EEOC v. Liggett* (1982), the court stated that in order to establish a prima facie case under the Equal Pay Act, the plaintiff must show that she receives less pay than a male coemployee performing work substantially equal in skill and responsibility under similar working conditions. They added that the comparison must be made factor by factor with the male comparator and that the plaintiff may not compare herself to a hypothetical male with a composite average of a group's skill, effort, and responsibility.

Two years later, the Fourth Circuit again affirmed a lower court's ruling in favor of the institution on an Equal Pay Act claim. In *Strag v. Board of Trustees, Craven Community College* (1995), the court cited Houck and said that the plaintiff must identify a particular male comparator for purposes of the inquiry and may not compare herself to a hypothetical of a composite male. Furthermore, the court held that in setting forth a prima facie case, isolated incidents or random comparisons demonstrating disparities in treatment may be insufficient to draw a prima facie inference of discrimination without additional evidence to support the claim.

Sometimes a claimant files under both the Equal Pay Act and Title VII because the coverage of gender overlaps between the two statutes. When members of the University of Washington nursing faculty filed pay disparity claims under both Title VII and the Equal Pay Act (*Spaulding v. University of Washington,* 1984), the Ninth Circuit affirmed the lower court's decision and held that the statistical analyses used by the plaintiffs did not support their claims. The court held that under the Title VII claim, the plaintiffs' statistics did not establish discriminatory intent on the part of the institution because the plaintiffs did not adequately account for prior job experience, rank, multiple degrees, or an evaluation of the actual work performed by the various faculty members. This occurred because plaintiffs did not use regression analysis, but rather used a matching technique and that "the more sophisticated the method of algebraic adjustment that is used . . . the more likely an illicit discriminatory factor can be ferreted out" (p. 704). They added that the difference in pay was primarily attributed to the fact that the women faculty held more jobs that traditionally paid lower than the types of jobs that the majority of the male faculty held, something for which multiple regression analyses may have been able to control.

In *Lavin-McEleney v. Marist College* (2001), the defendants appealed a jury verdict that awarded the plaintiff back pay, liquidated damages, and provided attorneys' fees and costs. In the district court trial, both parties presented regression analyses and, according to the appellate court, both were similar, and both found pay disparities between the plaintiff and comparable male professors. The major disagreement with the analyses was the disagreement between the two parties over the statistical significance of the difference. In addition to the first regression evidence provided by the defendant, they used another expert witness who performed a separate but similar regression analysis, as well as a content analysis to explain the relationship of the statistically supported results. The expert witness said that female professors were paid less because they chose to teach in disciplines that drew lower salaries in the national labor market.

The jury found for the defendant on the Equal Pay Act claim but decided that the institution's violation was not intentional to support the plaintiff's Title VII claim. The major thrust of the defendant's appeal concerned the way in which the comparator males were chosen. The plaintiff found it necessary to use the entire Marist faculty to establish a sufficiently large enough sample and then extrapolated from the model those professors who did not compare to the plaintiff across all variables of rank, years of service, division, tenure status, and degrees earned. The remainder of the male professors would be used to determine what they typically would have been paid. The appellate court held that regression analysis, based on a larger pool of male employees and that controlled for difference within each variable, properly supported the plaintiff's case and was appropriately employed to calculate damages.

Only two other professors were comparable to the plaintiff in each of the five categories identified by the expert witness. One was a woman who was the highest paid of the three, and the other was a male who, although higher paid than the plaintiff, was not paid higher than the other woman. Once a comparator male was established, the plaintiff created a statistical composite of all male faculty members in order to calculate damages. Marist objected to this method and cited both *Houck* and *Strag* to convince the court that the plaintiff must identify a particular male comparator for purposes of the inquiry and may not compare herself to a hypothetical of a composite male. The appellate court disagreed with the objection, stating that the plaintiff had effectively established a male comparator, but used the composite male average to calculate damages.

Sample Population. Two cases directly address the question concerning the inclusion of part-time faculty in a regression model. In *Coser* v. *Collvier* (1984), the Second Circuit affirmed the lower court's ruling that the plaintiff's regression analysis included the salaries of visiting faculty, lecturers, artists and performers, and other categories that, according to the judge, were not comparable to regular faculty. In *Bakewell* v. *Stephen F. Austin State University* (1996), the district court recognized that when the plaintiffs ran a regression analysis using the defendant's data that excluded part-time faculty and instructors, their case became less impressive. These rulings support current jurisprudence to the extent that although the "plaintiff may show that the jobs are substantially equal, not necessarily that they are identical" (*Spaulding* v. *University of Washington,* 1984, p. 697), part-time faculty positions may not be considered substantially equal in the eyes of the court. Furthermore, in the U.S. Supreme Court's decision in *Wards Cove Packing Co.* v. *Atonio* (1989), an imbalance in one segment of an employer's workforce is not sufficient to establish a prima facie case of disparate impact with respect to the selection of workers for the employer's other positions. This case clearly demonstrates that the gender disparity of part-time instructors or non-tenure-track faculty may not be sufficient to establish a prima facie case of gender disparity of full-time tenure-track faculty.

As to the question of including administrators, court decisions have varied. In general, if administrators are to be included in the analysis, the model must control for their administrative responsibility (*Presseisen* v. *Swarthmore College*, 1977; *Smith* v. *Virginia Commonwealth University*, 1996). In *Ottaviani* v. *State University of New York at New Paltz* (1989), the defendants criticized the plaintiff's statistical evidence on many grounds, including the fact that they did not properly account for faculty who had previously held full-time administrative appointments before returning to teaching at a higher pay. The lower court agreed and found that plaintiff's evidence failed to support claims of pay disparity. The Second Circuit Court of Appeals affirmed the lower court's decision.

Selection of Explanatory Variables. Within the courts, the choice of which explanatory variables to use when performing regression analysis has undergone intense debate. Probably the most significant case used to define variable selection in the courts is *Bazemore* v. *Friday* (1986). In this case, the U.S. Supreme Court found that the lower court erred when it concluded that the plaintiff's regression analysis was unacceptable because important factors were omitted from the model. The High Court held that a regression analysis that includes fewer than all measurable variables may still serve to prove a plaintiff's case and that the plaintiff does not have to prove discrimination with scientific certainty but by a preponderance of the evidence. In this case, the use of statistical evidence was overshadowed by legal reasoning and what the court deemed as common sense. Therefore, *Bazemore* set a standard by stating that while a regression model that does not contain all relevant variables may affect the probative value of the evidence, it should not affect its admissibility. Other court decisions, however, have fine-tuned this definition.

In *Penk* v. *Oregon State Board of Higher Education* (1987), the Ninth Circuit found that the plaintiff's regression model did not take into consideration important variables such as teaching quality, community and institutional service, and quality of research and scholarship. Citing *Bazemore,* the court said that the U.S. Supreme court did not give blanket approval to the introduction of all evidence derived from a regression analysis. However, in *Sobel* v. *Yeshiva University* (1988), the Second Circuit remanded the question of the validity of the regression analysis back to the lower court, stating that while the defendants objected to the plaintiff's analysis because it did not contain key variables, the defendant did not provide adequate proof to support such a claim.

In *Smith* v. *Virginia Commonwealth University* (1996), five male professors appealed a summary judgment claiming that raises given only to female faculty violated Title VII and the Equal Pay Act and that the regression analysis used by the university omitted key variables. The Fourth Circuit reversed the decision of the lower court and agreed with the appellants. It stated that although the institution considered the merit factors of teaching load, teaching quality, quantity and quality of publications, quantity and quality of research, and service to the community as part of its annual review, these factors were omitted from the university's regression analysis. Using *Bazemore* to buttress this finding, the court stated, "Bazemore and common sense require that any multiple regression analysis used to determine pay disparity must include all the major factors on which pay is determined" (p. 676).

In *Bickerstaff* v. *Vassar College* (1999), the plaintiffs' expert witness used a regression analysis that controlled for the independent variables of experience, rank, productivity, and discipline. The district court found that the statistical analysis did not control for teaching and service, even though Vassar determined its faculty merit points based on the criteria of scholarship, teaching, and service. The plaintiffs used the *Bazemore* case to argue that a regression analysis did not have to have all of the variables that explain salary variability. However, the court said that it rejected the plaintiffs' analysis not because it did not include all of the relevant variables; rather, it found that the evidence had little probative value because it omitted the major variables. Quoting *Bazemore,* the court found, "There may . . . be some regressions so incomplete as to be inadmissible as irrelevant" (p. 29). After these cases, there is little doubt that the courts have clearly distinguished between regression models that do not include all possible variables and those regression models that have omitted key variables. While the lower courts have not pulled away from the U.S. Supreme Court's decision in *Bazemore,* they have more narrowly defined it.

The court's reaction to the use of rank as an explanatory variable in regression analyses has changed throughout the years. In *Mecklenburg* v. *Montana Board of Regents of Higher Education* (1976), the court rejected the defendant's regression analysis because it included rank. In this case, the court believed that promotion might be based on discriminatory factors and therefore could not be used. In *Presseisen* v. *Swarthmore College* (1977), however, the court found that the plaintiff's regression analysis was unreliable because, among other things, the model failed to include rank. An expert witness for the plaintiff in *Ottaviani* v. *State University of New York at Paltz* (1989) ran more than one multiple regression analysis as evidence. Her main model did not include rank as a variable. She argued that academic rank was subject to discrimination at New Paltz and that the use of rank variables would therefore be inappropriate. The lower court found the argument unpersuasive and moved that a plaintiff had to prove that rank is tainted before it can be removed or not used in a regression model. In citing *Sobel* v. *Yeshiva University* (1988), the court stated, "Any regressions should include rank as a variable, while inclusion of any other contested variables will depend on the facts relevant to that variable" (p. 375).

NEW DIRECTIONS FOR INSTITUTIONAL RESEARCH • DOI: 10.1002/ir

The expert witness's second model in *Sobel* did include rank but combined instructors with assistant professors. The court agreed with the defendant's objection that when the two ranks were combined into a single one, the predicted salary of a female instructor would be based on the higher salary of an assistant professor. Therefore, the court concluded that the net residual difference between the predicted and actual salary of a female instructor would be overstated.

In *Bakewell* v. *Stephen F. Austin State University* (1996), the court found the plaintiff's regression models unsupportive of their claims because one of the models failed to include rank and the other used rank as a proxy to faculty performance. The court also stated that the plaintiff's models may suffer from multicollinearity because the experience, rank, degree, and gender variables could be significantly related to each other. The court did find that although there were questions concerning the reliability of the plaintiff's models, the problems were not enough to eviscerate the regression results of probative value.

The court found problems as well with the defendant's regression analysis because the institution used backward elimination and stepwise solutions to aid in model selection, which could be biased because the final model could be affected merely by changing the order by which the independent variables were removed or added. The court found too that the defendant's data suffered from error; when the defendants could not determine when a faculty member earned a master's degree, they made the assumption that it was conferred four years prior to earning the doctorate. Again, the court noted that, although the reliability of the model was questionable, "neither of these concerns robs the defendants' [model] of all probative value" (p. 898). In this case, neither side was able to establish a conclusive argument through regression analysis.

In some situations, rank has been used as a proxy in order to help account for performance. In theory, it is thought that the higher the rank obtained by faculty, the better the person had performed at teaching, research, and service. In *Smith* v. *Virginia Commonwealth University* (1996), the Fourth Circuit stated that although rank had to be included in a regression model, the use of rank as a "crude proxy" to determine productivity is subjective and is not suitable for statistical analysis. Similarly, in *Bakewell* v. *Stephen F. Austin State University* (1996), the district court cautioned against using rank as a proxy to determine faculty performance.

Another equally controversial area concerns the method by which different academic departments are accounted for, as well as the external market factors affecting how faculty within different disciplines are paid. In *Presseisen* v. *Swarthmore College* (1977), the court agreed with the defendant's expert witness, who testified that among other things, the plaintiff's regression analysis was unreliable because it did not account for different academic departments. The court recognized that although the regression analysis allowed different intersects, it did not allow the possibility of different slopes caused by different rates of changes of salaries from different departments. In *Wilkins* v. *University of Houston* (1981), the court ruled against the plaintiff because her regression model did not include a factor for discipline or market. In *Coser* v. *Collvier* (1984), the Second Circuit found that the plaintiff's regression analysis was not as conclusive as the defendant's because the institution's regression analysis compared faculty to each of Stony Brook's departments, while the plaintiff's study aggregated faculty into broader groups by fields of degree and used inconsistent aggregations. In contrast, the Second Circuit in *Lavin-McEleney* v. *Marist College* (2001) noted that both parties compared faculty salaries across divisions, not individual departments, although an expert witness for the institution claimed that the statistical difference in female salaries was caused by a "masked variable," the distinction between departments within each division.

In *Ende* v. *Board of Regents of Regency University* (1985), various male faculty members filed an Equal Pay Act claim against the university because the formula that the institution used to remedy confirmed salary disparities in women was unfair to male faculty. Although the Seventh Circuit affirmed the lower court's decision against the male faculty, it noted a weakness in the equity adjustment formula. According to the court, faculty members of any rank commanded less salary in some departments than in others because of marketplace factors. The court said, ". . . The University does not need to pay as much to attract and retain someone in the Department of Elementary Education as in the College of Business" (p. 180).

While the Second Circuit remanded *Sobel* v. *Yeshiva University* (1988) back to the lower court, it noted that the district court found the plaintiff's regression to be inadequate because it did not account for the disparities in salaries between faculty members in the higher-paid clinical departments and those of the lower-paid "preclinical" departments. While the higher court ordered the district court to use *Bazemore* v. *Friday* (1986) in determining the probative value of the plaintiff's regression model, the question as to whether academic departments should be accounted for remained for the lower court to decide.

Although past courts failed to address all of the questions raised by departmental or market variables used in faculty salary equity cases, parties on both sides have successfully used them in their regression models with very little contention. As future cases seek to define more narrowly comparable-worth factors using the Equal Pay Act, the need for the court to further address departmental and market differentials will become increasingly apparent.

Multiple Regression Procedures. The courts have also briefly examined the form in which a regression analysis is used. The majority of the current salary disparity cases in higher education involve the one-equation model (*Bazemore* v. *Friday*, 1986; *Wilkins* v. *University of Houston*, 1981; *Presseisen* v. *Swarthmore College*, 1977; *and Mecklenburg* v. *Montana Board of Regents of Higher Education*, 1976), while other cases have involved the two-equation approach (*Sobel* v. *Yeshiva University*, 1983).

Currently the courts have not decided if the single-model approach is stronger or weaker than the multiple-model approach. The court addressed a two-model approach in *Sobel* v. *Yeshiva University* (1988). In this case, the district court accepted the use of an approximation to a randomization test on the residuals of a standard linear regression to test the equality of two groups (referred to as an urn model), but the appellate court rejected it, stating that the model merely showed that the disparities could have occurred by chance, not that they actually did. Although the court did not state that a single model would have been better, the suggestion by Toutkoushian and Hoffman (2002) to use more than one model may have created a different outcome.

Statistical Significance. In general, the courts have recognized that when the results of statistical analysis yield levels of statistical significance at or below the .05 level, chance explanations for pay disparity become suspect. The U.S. Supreme Court held in *Hazelwood School District* v. *U.S.* (1977) that "where gross statistical disparities can be shown, they alone may in a proper case constitute a *prima facie* proof of a pattern of practice of discrimination" (p. 300). While most courts follow the conventions of social science and set the level of significance at .05 (*Frazier* v. *Consolidated Rail Corporation,* 1988), this is not considered an exact legal threshold (*Palmer* v. *George P. Shultz,* 1987). Again, although the courts recognize statistics as evidence, they may still lean toward legal reasoning and subjective analysis.

In *Griffin* v. *Board of Regents of Regency University* (1986), the Seventh Circuit observed that the lower court realized the difference between statistical and practical significance. According to the lower court, "For large samples, statistical significance at a level in the range below .05 or .01 is essentially equivalent to significance at the 2 to 3 standard deviation level." Although the acceptable level of practical significance has usually been set by the social sciences and the courts at 20 percent or above, it is interesting to note that in *Griffin,* the district court found that an R^2 square of .45 would not support an inference of discrimination because it considered the measure of determination too low. The plaintiffs argued that the use of R^2 leads to gross errors, and the appellate court agreed that the R^2 alone cannot determine the validity of a model. The court further said, "We recognize that sex discrimination may be present even though R^2 is low. However, the explanatory power of a regression is clearly relevant to the validity of the model" (p. 1296).

In *Presseisen* v. *Swarthmore College* (1977), the court considered another statistical argument. The plaintiff stated that the negative coefficient for women supported the contention that women's salaries on average were less than the expected average salaries for males. The plaintiff further stated that since this negative coefficient for women was apparent for five straight years, the probability of this happening five out of five times is less than .05. The defendant's expert witness disagreed: "[The] calculation that the probability, if there were no sex bias, of getting the same sign

NEW DIRECTIONS FOR INSTITUTIONAL RESEARCH • DOI: 10.1002/ir

five times in a row assumes, of course, that the observations being referred to are independent" (pp. 617–618). He added that because the databases for each of the five years contained many of the same people, this assumption could not be met. The court agreed with the defendant's assertion and found that the plaintiff's model was not adequate. This same argument was to resurface in *Bakewell* v. *Stephen F. Austin State University* (1996), when, citing *Presseisen*, the district court came to the same conclusion.

In conclusion, while the court has found problems with regression analysis, it has also come to expect at least some kind of statistical analysis from both sides in a salary disparity claim. In *Siler-Khodr* v. *University of Texas Health Science Center San Antonio* (2001), a statistical expert for the plaintiff used a multiple regression analysis that controlled for rank, degree, tenure, duration in the institution, and age. The analysis did not include a control for department. The university contended that the regression results were flawed because more women tended to be pediatricians than surgeons at medical schools across the country and that surgeons made significantly higher salaries than pediatricians. Furthermore, the institution claimed that the analysis did not analyze salaries within the OB/Gyn Department and mentioned nothing about the plaintiff's salary. The appellate court, citing *Bazemore* v. *Friday* (1986), stated that the plaintiff in a Title VII suit does not need to prove discrimination with scientific certainty; rather, the burden is to prove discrimination by a preponderance of the evidence.

What is noteworthy about this case is that both courts questioned why the institution failed to produce statistical evidence to rebut the analysis of the plaintiffs. Although the higher court stated that there were problems with the plaintiff's regression model, it affirmed the lower court's decision because of the lack of statistical evidence produced by the defendant.

Conclusion

It is important to regularly monitor faculty salaries in order to catch possible disparities, develop a fair and scientifically sound model that addresses the concerns of all parties involved, and ensure open communications between administrators and faculty in order to prevent lawsuits. Multiple regression analysis provides such a model to assess equitable compensation as an outcome of an institution's salary policies, from which salary inequities can be reduced on campus and future lawsuits can be prevented.

There is always a chance, however, that a lawsuit will follow such a study. Multiple regression analysis has become an increasingly important tool in assessing pay as more faculty gender pay disparity cases go before the courts with increased reliance of statistical evidence by both parties in order to establish or contest a prima facie case of discrimination. Gender discrimination is a legal issue, and legal decisions have affected how future salary disparity cases may be tried. Many of these decisions involve the type of statistical analysis to be used, the definition of statistical significance, and the variables that should be used in appropriate statistical models. Therefore, it is important that administrators and faculty understand both the statistical science and legal precedent of salary equity models so that the institution can develop a regression model that is statistically valid and legally sound. Multiple regression analysis can also be used to determine compensation and calculate damages during settlement proceedings.

There is a set of key assumptions that should be met before the results of any regression analysis can be considered for a study or in court, including reliable data and a correctly specified model. Violating these key assumptions will render the regression results invalid and potentially inadmissible by the courts.

References

Bakewell v. Stephen F. Austin State University, 975 F. Supp. 858 (1996).

Balzer, W., and others. "Critical Modeling Principles When Testing for Gender Equity in Faculty Salary." *Research in Higher Education,* 1996, 37(6), 633–658.

Bazemore v. Friday, 487 U.S. 385 (1986).

Bickerstaff v. Vassar College, 196 F.3d 435 (1999).

Bohannon, T. "Applying Regression Analysis to Problems in Institutional Research." In B. Yancy (ed.), *Applying Statistics in Institutional Research.* San Francisco: Jossey-Bass, 1988.

Boudreau, N., and others. "Should Faculty Rank Be Included as a Predictor Variable in Studies of Gender Equity in University Faculty Salaries?" *Research in Higher Education,* 1997, 38(3) 297–312.

Braskamp, L., Muffo, J., and Langston, I. "Determining Salary Equity: Politics, Procedures, and Problems." *Journal of Higher Education,* 1978, 49, 231–246.

Chronister, J., Ganeneder, B., Harper, E., and Baldwin, R. "Full-Time Non-Tenure-Track Faculty: Gender Differences." *NEA Higher Education Research Center Update,* 1997, 3(5), 1–4.

Coser v. Collvier, 739 F.2d 746 (1984).

EEOC v. Liggett, 690 F.2d 1072 (1982).

Ende v. Board of Regents of Regency University, 757 F.2d 176 (1985).

Equal Pay Act, 29 U.S.C. sec. 206(d) (1964).

Finkelstein, M., and Levin, B. *Statistics for Lawyers.* New York: Springer-Verlag, 1990.

Fisher, F. "Multiple Regression in Legal Proceedings." *Columbia Law Review,* 1980, 80, 702–736.

Frazier v. Consolidated Rail Corporation, 851 F.2d 1447 (1988).

Gilmartin, K., and Hartka, E. "Using Regression Analysis to Compute Back Pay." *Jurimetrics Journal of Law, Science and Technology,* 1991, 31(3), 289–317.

Gray, M. "Can Statistics Tell Us What We Do Not Want to Hear? The Case of Complex Salary Structures." *Statistical Science,* 1993, 8, 144–179.

Griffin v. Board of Regents of Regency University, 795 F.2d 1281 (1986).

Gujarati, D. *Basic Econometrics.* New York: Irwin/McGraw-Hill, 2003.

Haignere, L. *Paychecks: A Guide to Conducting Salary-Equity Studies for Higher Education.* Washington, D.C.: American Association of University Professors, 2002.

Hamermesh, D. "Not So Bad: The Annual Report on the Economic Status of the Profession." *Academe,* 1996, 82, 14–108.

Hazelwood School District v. U.S., 433 U.S. 399 (1977).

Houck v. Virginia Polytechnic Institute and State University, 10 F.3d 204 (1993).

International Brotherhood of Teamsters v. U.S., 431 U.S. 324 (1977).

Kennedy, P. *A Guide to Econometrics*. Ames, Iowa: Blackwell, 2003.

Lavin-McEleney v. Marist College, 239 F.3d 476 (2001).

Luna, A. "Faculty Salary Equity Studies: Combining Statistics with the Law." *Journal of Higher Education, 2006, 77*(2), 193–244.

Maddala, G. *Introduction to Econometrics*. Hoboken, N.J.: Wiley, 2001.

McDonnell Douglas Corp. v. Green, 411 U.S. 792 (1973).

McLaughlin, G., and Howard, R. "Faculty Salary Analyses." In W. Knight (ed.), *The Primer for Institutional Research*. Tallahassee, Fla.: Association for Institutional Research, 2003.

McLaughlin, G., Smart, J., and Montgomery, J. "Factors Which Comprise Salary." *Research in Higher Education, 1978, 8*, 67–82.

Mecklenburg v. Montana Board of Regents of Higher Education, 93 Empl. Prac. Dec. 11, 438 (D. Mont. 1976).

Ottaviani v. State University of New York at New Paltz, 875 F.2d 365 (1989).

Palmer v. George P. Shultz, 815 F.2d 84 (1987).

Penk v. Oregon State Board of Higher Education, 816 F.2d (1987).

Presseisen v. Swarthmore College, 422 F. Supp. 593 (1977).

Siler-Khodr v. The University of Texas Health Science Center San Antonio, 261 F.3d 542 (2001).

Smith v. Virginia Commonwealth University, 84 F.3d 672 (1996).

Snyder, J., Hyer, P., and McLaughlin, G. "Faculty Salary Equity: Issues and Options." *Research in Higher Education, 1994, 35*, 1–19.

Sobel v. Yeshiva University, 839 F.2d 18 (1988).

Spaulding v. University of Washington, 740 F.2d 686 (1984).

Strag v. Board of Trustees, Craven Community College, 55 F.3d 943 (1995).

Toutkoushian, R. (ed.). *Conducting Salary-Equity Studies: Alternative Approaches to Research*. New Directions for Institutional Research, no. 115. San Francisco: Jossey-Bass, 2002.

Toutkoushian, R. (ed.). *Unresolved Issues in Conducting Salary-Equity Studies*. New Directions for Institutional Research, no. 117. San Francisco: Jossey-Bass, 2003.

Toutkoushian, R., and Hoffman, E. "Alternatives for Measuring the Unexplained Wage Gap." In R. Toutkoushian (ed.), *Conducting Salary-Equity Studies: Alternative Approaches to Research*. New Directions for Institutional Research, no. 115. San Francisco: Jossey-Bass, 2002.

Wards Cove Packing Co. v. Atonio, 490 U.S. 642 (1989).

Webster, A. "Demographic Factors Affecting Faculty Salary." *Educational and Psychological Measurement, 1995, 55*(5), 728–735.

Wilkins v. University of Houston, 654 F.2d 388 (1981).

JULIE A. FRIZELL *is an economist at the Washington, D.C., office of ERS Group.*

BENJAMIN S. SHIPPEN JR. *is an economist at the Tallahassee, Florida, office of ERS Group.*

ANDREW L. LUNA *is director of institutional research, planning, and assessment at the University of North Alabama.*

NEW DIRECTIONS FOR INSTITUTIONAL RESEARCH • DOI: 10.1002/ir

INDEX

classroom attributes with student learning success. With twenty-first-century technology, facilities data is useful far beyond traditional business affairs operations—it has become integral to institutional planning and operation.
ISBN: 978-04702-55254

IR134   **Advancing Sustainability in Higher Education**
Larry H. Litten, Dawn Geronimo Terkla
Effective organizations strive constantly to improve. Colleges and universities are becoming increasingly aware of financial, social, and environmental challenges—both to their continued well-being and to the societies they serve—many of which are subsumed under the category of sustainability. In order to maintain progress, manage risk, and conserve resources, policymakers and managers need information that monitors performance, illuminates risk, and demonstrates responsible institutional behavior. Institutional researchers bring distinctive knowledge and skills to the table. This volume of *New Directions for Institutional Research* identifies various obstacles to sustainable progress and describes solutions for advancing educational institutions and the societies in which they are embedded.
ISBN: 978-04701-76870

IR133   **Using Quantitative Data to Answer Critical Questions**
Frances K. Stage
This volume of *New Directions for Institutional Research* challenges quantitative researchers to become more critical. By providing examples from the work of several prominent researchers, and by offering concrete recommendations, the editor and authors deliver messages that are likely to cause many educational researchers to reexamine their own work. The collective efforts described here will help readers become more sensitive to the nuances among various educational groups, and to pay more attention to outliers. This volume supplies both motivation and analytical support to those who might incorporate criticality into their own quantitative work, as well as to those who wish to read critical perspectives with an open mind about what they might find.
ISBN: 978-07879-97786

IR132   **Applying Economics to Institutional Research**
Robert K. Toutkoushian, Michael B. Paulsen
In many ways, economic concepts, models, and methods can be applied to higher education research. This volume's chapter authors are all higher education researchers with graduate training in economics and extensive experience in institutional research. They share insight on the economist's perspective of education costs and revenues, plus how to use economics to inform enrollment management and to understand faculty labor market issues.
ISBN: 978-07879-95768

IR131   **Data Mining in Action: Case Studies of Enrollment Management**
Jing Luan, Chun-Mei Zhao
Data mining has great potential to enhance institutional research. Six case studies in this volume employed data mining for solving real-world problems in enrollment yield, retention, transfer-outs, utilization of advanced-placement scores, predicting graduation rates, and more. Discusses data mining vs. traditional statistics, debunks the myths, and highlights the need for individual pattern recognition and customized treatment of students.
ISBN: 0-7879-9426-X

IR130 **Reframing Persistence Research to Improve Academic Success**
Edward P. St. John, Michael Wilkerson
This volume proposes and tests new collaborations between institutional researchers and others on campus who are engaged in breaking down barriers to academic success, especially for minorities and nontraditional students. What if traditional recommendations aren't effective? Chapters review prior research and best practices, then investigate new approaches to assessment, action research, action inquiry, and evaluation. Lessons learned can inform strategies of administrators, faculty, and everyone interested in improving success for all students.
ISBN: 0-7879-8759-X

IR129 **Analyzing Faculty Work and Rewards: Using Boyer's Four Domains of Scholarship**
John M. Braxton
Boyer's four domains—scholarships of discovery, application, integration, and teaching—influence and define scholars as their professional roles, career stages, and research goals change. This volume offers practical suggestions for academic reward structure, graduate school preparation, and state policy.
ISBN: 0-7879-8674-7

IR128 **Workforce Development and Higher Education: A Strategic Role for Institutional Research**
Richard A. Voorhees, Lee Harvey
Workforce development is a growing area for higher education. This volume examines its conceptual underpinnings from an international perspective, and it provides practical institutional case studies and specific techniques for gauging the market potential for new instructional programs. It discusses suggested projects and studies for IR personnel to consider on their campuses.
ISBN: 0-7879-8365-9

IR127 **Survey Research: Emerging Issues**
Paul D. Umbach
Demands for accountability are forcing colleges and universities to conduct more high-quality surveys to gauge institutional effectiveness. New technologies are improving survey implementation as well as researchers' ability to effectively analyze data. This volume examines these emerging issues in a rapidly changing environment and highlights lessons learned from past research.
ISBN: 0-7879-8329-2

IR126 **Enhancing Alumni Research: European and American Perspectives**
David J. Weerts, Javier Vidal
The increasing globalization of higher education has made it easy to compare problems, goals, and tools associated with conducting alumni research worldwide. This research is also being used to learn about the impact, purposes, and successes of higher education. This volume will help institutional leaders use alumni research to respond to the increasing demands of state officials, accrediting agencies, employers, prospective students, parents, and the general public.
ISBN: 0-7879-8228-8

IR125 **Minority Retention: What Works?**
Gerald H. Gaither
Examines some of the best policies, practices, and procedures to achieve greater diversity and access, while controlling costs and maintaining quality.

Looks at institutions that are majority-serving, tribal, Hispanic-serving, and historically black. Emphasizes that the key to retention is in the professional commitment of faculty and staff to student-centered efforts, and includes practical ideas adaptable to different institutional goals.
ISBN: 0-7879-7974-0

IR124   **Unique Campus Contexts: Insights for Research and Assessment**
Jason E. Lane, M. Christopher Brown II
Summarizes what we know about professional schools, transnational campuses, proprietary schools, religious institutions, and corporate universities. As more students take advantage of these specialized educational environments, conducting meaningful research becomes a challenge. The authors argue for the importance of educational context and debunk the one-size-fits-all approach to assessment, evaluation, and research. Effective institutional measures of inquiry, benchmarks, and indicators must be congruent with the mission, population, and function of each unique campus context.
ISBN: 0-7879-7973-2

IR123   **Successful Strategic Planning**
Michael J. Dooris, John M. Kelley, James F. Trainer
Explains the value of strategic planning in higher education to improve conditions and meet missions (hiring better faculty, recruiting stronger students, upgrading facilities, improving programs, acquiring resources), and what planning tools and methodologies have been used at various campuses. Goes beyond the activity of planning to investigate successful ways to implement and infuse strategic plans throughout the organization. Case studies from various campuses show different ways to achieve success.
ISBN: 0-7879-7792-6

IR122   **Assessing Character Outcomes in College**
Jon C. Dalton, Terrence R. Russell, Sally Kline
Examines several perspectives on the role of higher education in developing students' character, and illustrates approaches to defining and assessing character outcomes. Moral, civic, ethical, and spiritual development are key aspects of students' growth and experience in college, so how can educators encourage good values and assess their impact?
ISBN: 0-7879-7791-8

IR121   **Overcoming Survey Research Problems**
Stephen R. Porter
As demand for survey research has increased, survey response rates have decreased. This volume examines an array of survey research problems and best practices, from both the literature and field practitioners, to provide solutions to increase response rates while controlling costs. Discusses administering longitudinal studies, doing surveys on sensitive topics such as student drug and alcohol use, and using new technologies for survey administration.
ISBN: 0-7879-7477-3

IR120   **Using Geographic Information Systems in Institutional Research**
Daniel Teodorescu
Exploring the potential of geographic information systems (GIS) applications in higher education administration, this issue introduces IR professionals and campus administrators to a powerful presentation and analysis tool. Chapters explore the benefits of working with the spatial component of data in recruitment, admissions, facilities, alumni development, and other areas, with examples of actual GIS applications from several higher education institutions.
ISBN: 0-7879-7281-9

IR119　**Maximizing Revenue in Higher Education**
F. King Alexander, Ronald G. Ehrenberg
This volume presents edited versions of some of the best articles from a forum on institutional revenue generation sponsored by the Cornell Higher Education Research Institute. The chapters provide different perspectives on revenue generation and how institutions are struggling to find an appropriate balance between meeting public expectations and maximizing private market forces. The insights provided about options and alternatives will enable campus leaders, institutional researchers, and policymakers to better understand evolving patterns in public and private revenue reliance.
ISBN: 0-7879-7221-5

IR118　**Studying Diverse Institutions: Contexts, Challenges, and Considerations**
M. Christopher Brown II, Jason E. Lane
This volume examines the contextual and methodological issues pertaining to studying diverse institutions (including women's colleges, tribal colleges, and military academies), and provides effective and useful approaches for higher education administrators, institutional researchers and planners, policymakers, and faculty seeking to better understand students in postsecondary education. It also offers guidelines to asking the right research questions, employing the appropriate research design and methods, and analyzing the data with respect to the unique institutional contexts.
ISBN: 0-7879-6990-7

IR117　**Unresolved Issues in Conducting Salary-Equity Studies**
Robert K. Toutkoushian
Chapters discuss the issues surrounding how to use faculty rank, seniority, and experience as control variables in salary-equity studies. Contributors review the challenges of conducting a salary-equity study for nonfaculty administrators and staff—who constitute the majority of employees, even in academic institutions—and examine the advantages and disadvantages of using hierarchical linear modeling to measure pay equity. They present a case-study approach to illustrate the political and practical challenges that researchers often face when conducting a salary-equity study for an institution. This is a companion volume to *Conducting Salary-Equity Studies: Alternative Approaches to Research* (IR115).
ISBN: 0-7879-6863-3

IR116　**Reporting Higher Education Results: Missing Links in the Performance Chain**
Joseph C. Burke, Henrick P. Minassians
The authors review performance reporting's coverage, content, and customers, they examine in depth the reporting indicators, types, and policy concerns, and they compare them among different states' reports. They highlight weaknesses in our current performance reporting—such as a lack of comparable indicators for assessing the quality of undergraduate education—and make recommendations about how to best use and improve performance information.
ISBN: 0-7879-6336-4

IR115　**Conducting Salary-Equity Studies: Alternative Approaches to Research**
Robert K. Toutkoushian
Synthesizing nearly 30 years of research on salary equity from the field of economics and the experiences of past studies, this issue launches an important dialogue between scholars and institutional researchers on the methodology and application of salary-equity studies in today's higher education institutions. The first of a two-volume set on the subject, it also bridges the gap between

academic research and the more pragmatic statistical and political considerations in real-life institutional salary studies.
ISBN: 0-7879-6335-6

IR114   **Evaluating Faculty Performance**
Carol L. Colbeck
This issue brings new insights to faculty work and its assessment in light of reconsideration of faculty work roles, rapid technological change, increasing bureaucratization of the core work of higher education, and public accountability for performance. Exploring successful methods that individuals, institutions, and promotion and tenure committees are using for evaluations of faculty performance for career development, this issue is an indispensable guide to academic administrators and institutional researchers involved in the faculty evaluation process.
ISBN: 0-7879-6334-8

IR113   **Knowledge Management: Building a Competitive Advantage in Higher Education**
Andreea M. Serban, Jing Luan
Provides a comprehensive discussion of knowledge management, covering its theoretical, practical, and technological aspects with an emphasis on their relevance for applications in institutional research. Chapters examine the theoretical basis and impact of data mining; discuss the role of institutional research in customer relationship management; and provide a framework for the integration of institutional research within the larger context of organization learning. With a synopsis of technologies that support knowledge management and an exploration of future developments in this field, this volume assists institutional researchers and analysts in taking advantage of the opportunities of knowledge management and addressing its challenges.
ISBN: 0-7879-6291-0

IR112   **Balancing Qualitative and Quantitative Information for Effective Decision Support**
Richard D. Howard, Kenneth W. Borland Jr.
Establishes methods for integration of numeric data and its contextual application. With theoretical and practical examples, contributors explore the techniques and realities of creating, communicating, and using balanced decision support information. Chapters discuss the critical role of measurement in building institutional quality; examples of conceptual and theoretical frameworks and their application for the creation of evaluation information; and methods of communicating data and information in relation to its decision support function.
ISBN: 0-7879-5796-8

IR111   **Higher Education as Competitive Enterprise: When Markets Matter**
Robert Zemsky, Susan Shaman, Daniel B. Shapiro
Offers a comprehensive history of the development and implementation of Collegiate Results Instrument (CRI), a tool for mapping the connection between market forces and educational outcomes in higher education. Chapters detail the methods that CRI uses to help institutions to remain value centered by becoming market smart.
ISBN: 0-7879-5795-X

IR110   **Measuring What Matters: Competency-Based Learning Models in Higher Education**
Richard Voorhees
An analysis of the findings of the National Postsecondary Education Cooperative project on data and policy implications of national skill standards, this issue

provides researchers, faculty, and academic administrators with the tools needed to deal effectively with the emerging competency-based initiatives.
ISBN: 0-7879-1411-8

IR109 **The Student Ratings Debate: Are They Valid? How Can We Best Use Them?**
Michael Theall, Philip C. Abrami, Lisa A. Mets
Presents a thorough analysis of the use of student evaluations of teaching for summative decisions and discusses the ongoing controversies, emerging research, and dissenting opinions on their utility and validity. Summarizes the role of student ratings as tools for instructional improvement, as evidence for promotion and tenure decisions, as the means for student course selection, as a criterion of program effectiveness, and as the continuing focus of active research and intensive discussion.
ISBN: 0-7879-5756-9

IR108 **Collaboration Between Student Affairs and Institutional Researchers to Improve Institutional Effectiveness**
J. Worth Pickering, Gary R. Hanson
Defines the unique aspects of student affairs research, including its role in responding to assessment mandates and accreditation agencies, its use of student development theory in formulating research questions, the value of qualitative methods it employs, and the potential contribution it can make to institutional decision making.
ISBN: 0-7879-5727-5

IR107 **Understanding the College Choice of Disadvantaged Students**
Alberto F. Cabrera, Steven M. La Nasa
Examines the college-choice decision of minority and disadvantaged students and suggests avenues to help promote access and improve participation. Explores the influence of family and high school variables as well as racial and ethnic differences on college-choice.
ISBN: 0-7879-5439-X

IR106 **Analyzing Costs in Higher Education: What Institutional Researchers Need to Know**
Michael F. Middaugh
Presents both the conceptual and practical information that will give researchers solid grounding in selecting the best approach to cost analysis. Offers an overview of cost studies covering basic issues and beyond, from a review of definitions of expenditure categories and rules of financial reporting to a discussion of a recent congressionally mandated study of higher education costs.
ISBN: 0-7879-5437-3

NEW DIRECTIONS FOR INSTITUTIONAL RESEARCH
Order Form
SUBSCRIPTIONS AND SINGLE ISSUES

DISCOUNTED BACK ISSUES:

Use this form to receive **20% off** all back issues of New Directions for Institutional Research. All single issues priced at **$23.20** (normally $29.00)

TITLE	ISSUE NO.	ISBN
_____	_____	_____
_____	_____	_____
_____	_____	_____

Call 888-378-2537 or see mailing instructions below. When calling, mention the promotional code, JB7ND, to receive your discount.

SUBSCRIPTIONS: *(1 year, 4 issues)*

☐ New Order   ☐ Renewal

U.S.	☐ Individual: $80	☐ Institutional: $185
Canada/Mexico	☐ Individual: $80	☐ Institutional: $225
All Others	☐ Individual: $104	☐ Institutional: $269

Call 888-378-2537 or see mailing and pricing instructions below. Online subscriptions are available at www.interscience.wiley.com.

Copy or detach page and send to:
John Wiley & Sons, Journals Dept, 5th Floor
989 Market Street, San Francisco, CA 94103-1741

Order Form can also be faxed to: 888-481-2665

Issue/Subscription Amount: $ _____
Shipping Amount: $ _____
(for single issues only—subscription prices include shipping)
Total Amount: $ _____

SHIPPING CHARGES:

SURFACE	Domestic	Canadian
First Item	$5.00	$6.00
Each Add'l Item	$3.00	$1.50

(No sales tax for U.S. subscriptions. Canadian residents, add GST for subscription orders. Individual rate subscriptions must be paid by personal check or credit card. Individual rate subscriptions may not be resold as library copies.)

☐ Payment enclosed (U.S. check or money order only. All payments must be in U.S. dollars.)

☐ VISA ☐ MC ☐ Amex # _____ Exp. Date _____

Card Holder Name _____ Card Issue # _____

Signature _____ Day Phone _____

☐ Bill Me (U.S. institutional orders only. Purchase order required.)

Purchase order # _____
Federal Tax ID13559302   GST 89102 8052

Name _____

Address _____

Phone _____ E-mail _____

JB7ND

Complete online access for your institution

A PUBLICATION OF THE SCHOOL OF ADVANCED STUDIES OF UNIVERSITY OF PHOENIX

JOURNAL OF LEADERSHIP STUDIES

Expanding Interdisciplinary Discourse

SPRING 2008   VOLUME 2   ISSUE 1

The Role of Organizational Cultures in Information-Systems Security Management:
A Goal-Setting Perspective
Ioannis V. Koskosas, Georgia Charitoudi, and Malamati Louta

A Conscious-Authentic Leadership Approach in the Workplace:
Leading From Within
Robert E. Hofman, Jr.

Utilizing Cool Posing Narrative and Technique as Leadership Strategies Among
Underrepresented Individuals
George M. Crase, III

Register for complimentary online access to *Journal of Leadership Studies* today!

WILEY
Publishers Since 1807

WILEY
InterScience®
DISCOVER SOMETHING GREAT